Preface

This monograph originated with a Smith Richardson Foundation research grant to explore the question of how unofficial regional security dialogues affect security perceptions and policy in regions defined by conflict. Do such dialogues affect adversarial relationships and, if so, how? What are the limits and dangers of such dialogues? The growing importance of regional contexts and nonstate actors in addressing a multitude of conflicts has created a greater demand for unofficial track two security dialogues as a critical foreign policy tool. The appeal of unofficial dialogues is their ability to raise ideas and solutions that might not be possible in official circles, but that could over time influence official thinking and, ultimately, policy. What seems unthinkable today may, through unofficial contacts, become the norm tomorrow.

But such assumptions about the power of track two diplomacy have rarely been systematically assessed through empirical analysis. This work is an attempt to do so. Through an examination of regional security track two efforts in the Middle East and South Asia, this monograph considers the roles as well as the limits of such processes and offers ways in which project organizers and funders might assess various efforts. Such assessments can provide not only a better understanding of what these types of dialogues have or have not accomplished in the past, but also a framework for understanding and improving these efforts in the future. The findings and lessons of this work should apply not only to the Middle East and South Asia, but also to other regions struggling to resolve long-standing adversarial relationships.

This monograph expands and updates previous work the author has conducted in the area of track two diplomacy, including *Rethinking Track Two Diplomacy: The Middle East and South Asia* (Kaye, 2005) and "Track Two Diplomacy and Regional Security in the Middle East" (Kaye, 2001b).

This work should be of interest to members of security policy communities in the United States and abroad as well as regional experts focusing specifically on the Middle East and South Asia. Academic researchers and teachers of courses on conflict resolution may also find the monograph useful. Finally, the work should be helpful to the many private foundations that fund regional track two efforts as they attempt to assess the returns on their investment. Comments are welcome and should be directed to the author (Dalia_Kaye@rand.org).

This monograph results from the RAND Corporation's continuing program of self-initiated independent research. Support for such research is provided, in part, by donors and by the independent research and development provisions of RAND's contracts for the operation of its U.S. Department of Defense federally funded research and development centers.

RAND's National Security Research Division (NSRD) oversaw the final stages of this research.

This research was conducted within the International Security and Defense Policy Center (ISDP) of the RAND National Security Research Division (NSRD). NSRD conducts research and analysis for the Office of the Secretary of Defense, the Joint Staff, the Unified Combatant Commands, the defense agencies, the Department of the Navy, the Marine Corps, the U.S. Coast Guard, the U.S. Intelligence Community, allied foreign governments, and foundations.

For more information on RAND's International Security and Defense Policy Center, contact the Director, James Dobbins. He can be reached by email at James_Dobbins@rand.org; by phone at 703-413-1100, extension 5134; or by mail at the RAND Corporation, 1200 South Hayes Street, Arlington, Virginia 22202-5050. More information about RAND is available at www.rand.org.

Talking to the Enemy

Track Two Diplomacy in the Middle East and South Asia

Dalia Dassa Kaye

 NATIONAL SECURITY RESEARCH DIVISION

This research was conducted within the International Security and Defense Policy Center (ISDP) of the RAND National Security Research Division (NSRD). NSRD conducts research and analysis for the Office of the Secretary of Defense, the Joint Staff, the Unified Commands, the defense agencies, the Department of the Navy, the Marine Corps, the U.S. Coast Guard, the U.S. Intelligence Community, allied foreign governments, and foundations.

Library of Congress Cataloging-in-Publication Data

Kaye, Dalia Dassa.
    Talking to the enemy : track two diplomacy in the Middle East and South Asia / Dalia Dassa Kaye.
      p. cm.
    Includes bibliographical references.
    ISBN 978-0-8330-4191-3 (pbk. : alk. paper)
    1. Conflict management—Case studies. 2. Arab-Israeli conflict—1993——Peace. 3. Conflict management—South Asia. 4. Mediation, International. 5. Security, International. I. Title.

    JZ6368.K394 2007
    956.05'3—dc22

    2007028637

The RAND Corporation is a nonprofit research organization providing objective analysis and effective solutions that address the challenges facing the public and private sectors around the world. RAND's publications do not necessarily reflect the opinions of its research clients and sponsors.

RAND® is a registered trademark.

Cover Design by Stephen Bloodsworth

Published 2007 by the RAND Corporation
1776 Main Street, P.O. Box 2138, Santa Monica, CA 90407-2138
1200 South Hayes Street, Arlington, VA 22202-5050
4570 Fifth Avenue, Suite 600, Pittsburgh, PA 15213-2665
RAND URL: http://www.rand.org/
To order RAND documents or to obtain additional information, contact
Distribution Services: Telephone: (310) 451-7002;
Fax: (310) 451-6915; Email: order@rand.org

Contents

Figure and Tables

Figure

Tables

Summary

Key Questions

How do adversaries manage to sit down and talk about long-standing conflicts while violence and mistrust continue to define their security relations? While official diplomatic communications are the obvious way for adversaries to talk, unofficial policy discourse, or track two diplomacy, is an increasingly important part of the changing international security landscape. Private foundations, nongovernmental organizations (NGOs), universities, and governments—mostly based in the West—have devoted significant financial and human resources to track two dialogues. What has been the payoff?

The experiences of the Middle East and South Asia suggest that track two regional security dialogues rarely lead to dramatic policy shifts or the resolution of long-standing conflicts. But they have played a significant role in shaping the views, attitudes, and knowledge of elites, both civilian and military, and in some instances have begun to affect security policy. However, any notable influence on policy from such efforts is likely to be long-term, due to the nature of the activity and the constraints of carrying out such discussions in regions vastly different from the West.

As a result, we need to set realistic expectations about what track two can accomplish. Track two dialogues on regional security are less about producing diplomatic breakthroughs than socializing an influential group of elites to think in cooperative ways. Track two dialogues can alter views about the value of cooperation with other regional actors, even if attitudes toward those actors remain generally negative.

Such dialogue serves as a conditioning process in which regional actors are exposed to new concepts, adapt them to their own contexts, and shape policy debates over time.

The reframing of security perceptions and postures gains more traction when regional elites view such change as in their own interests, not as a favor to external actors. Making track two dialogues an indigenous process is thus crucial for their success. Without adaptation to local environments, track two supporters who attempt to sell and spread track two ideas to their own governments and societies will have difficulty being viewed as legitimate.

Track two dialogues typically involve moderate and pragmatic voices that have the potential to wield positive influence in volatile environments, and the stakes are high. Greater understanding of track two dialogues should lead to less skepticism of such activities and a concerted investment in and careful promotion of these efforts.

Track Two Roles and Limits

This study identifies three conceptual stages that define the evolution of track two dialogues, although in practice these stages are not necessarily sequential: socialization, filtering, and policy adjustment.

During socialization, outside experts, often from Western governments or nongovernmental institutions, organize forums to share security concepts and lessons based on experiences from their own regions. This stage focuses on encouraging a small group of influential elites—including those from the military—to think differently about regional security and the value of cooperation, providing new terms of reference and information about specific security issues. Socialization also attempts to limit misperceptions and inaccurate assumptions about regional neighbors or important extraregional actors.

Filtering involves widening the constituency favoring regional cooperation beyond a select number of policy elites involved in track two, through the media, parliament, NGOs, education systems, and citizen interest groups. In practice, this stage has often been the weak link in track two dialogues, as there has been inconsistent translation of the ideas developed in regional security dialogues to groups outside the socialized circle of elites.

The final stage is the transmission of the ideas fostered in dialogues to tangible shifts in security policy, such as altered military and security doctrines or new regional arms control regimes or political agreements. Track two has not led to such extensive shifts in security policy, although there are examples of track two work influencing official thinking and a variety of security initiatives and activities, particularly in South Asia.

A number of limitations—at the individual, domestic, and regional levels—explain why many track two efforts never reach their full potential. Individuals participating in track two dialogues may be ideological and opposed to cooperation with an adversary. Regional participants may also enter such dialogues with skeptical or hostile positions because they come from security cultures that are adverse to cooperative security ideas. Mainstream positions in regions such as the Middle East and South Asia favor unilateralist, self-help thinking. Indeed, interactions in track two dialogues have, in some cases, led participants to develop views of their adversary that are more rather than less negative. Others may simply fail to buy in to cooperative security concepts.

Another problem with participants may be that even if organizers find individuals who are open-minded to new security relationships and frameworks, these participants may have limited influence with official policymakers and may be disconnected from grassroots groups or other broadly based societal movements. Because track two is a long-term investment, organizers must consider including a wide range of participants—even those initially hostile to the process—because of the possibility that some of these participants may later assume important official positions in their countries.

Domestic factors also can create impediments to progress in track two dialogues. Cooperative security ideas are not popular among populations that have experienced long-standing conflicts and high levels of violence. Cooperative postures are particularly dangerous for vulnerable regimes lacking legitimacy, because domestic opposition groups can use new security policies favoring cooperation with an adversary as political ammunition against a regime, particularly if such policy shifts are associated with Western agendas. We see great sensitivity to publicizing track two dialogues in the Middle East for this reason.

Finally, the regional environment can affect calculations about whether track two efforts can be introduced to a larger audience. Generally, in more favorable security environments—such as when official peace processes dealing with core bilateral conflicts like Kashmir or Israel-Palestine appear to be moving forward—there is a greater chance for the development of an elite constituency favoring regional security cooperation and for exposure and acceptance at the broader societal level. Conversely, high levels of regional conflict and tension make the transmission of cooperative security ideas to official policymakers and the wider public more difficult. This of course raises the dilemma that when unofficial channels may be most needed, they may be most difficult to bring about.

Key Middle East Findings

Track two dialogues in the Middle East have affected growing numbers of regional elites. Approximately 750 regional and extraregional elites participated in track two activities during the 1990s, of which an estimated 200 were from the military. Today, thousands of individuals have participated in one or more track two activities related to the Middle East. During the 1990s, approximately 100 track two events were organized, averaging one activity per month. Although the pace has slowed for broader regional forums, more recent track two activism in the Gulf suggests that frequent and regular track two activities continue.

But Middle East dialogues are changing. The lack of progress on the Israeli-Palestinian track has made unofficial dialogues among Arabs and Israelis more difficult. The tense regional environment has slowed progress on cooperative Arab-Israeli initiatives and increased the stakes for participants. Arab-Israeli–oriented track two groups thus find it increasingly challenging to meet in the region and to attract sufficient funding. Some of the most prominent groups could not have survived without funding from the U.S. government or other, largely Western, extraregional actors.

Because of these difficulties, over the past several years Middle East track two forums have downplayed Arab-Israeli issues and instead focused on other challenges, particularly Gulf security and Iran. Some track two forums are originating in the Gulf, suggesting a new confidence among Gulf Cooperation Council (GCC) actors in asserting their interests in forums separate from the broader Arab agenda, which is traditionally led by key Arab states such as Egypt.

What have these dialogues achieved over the years? Their socialization function has succeeded in shaping a core and not-insignificant number of security elites across the region to begin thinking and speaking with a common vocabulary. For example, senior Iranian advisors have given talks that directly mirror the language of cooperative security promoted by various Middle East groups. Similarly, high-level Egyptian officials have given speeches referencing track two ideas. Track two concepts influenced sections of the official Israeli-Jordan peace treaty. And new efforts have sprung up in the Gulf in recent years, leading to new regional security communities increasingly thinking in cooperative terms. For instance, the idea of a Gulf weapons of mass destruction free zone promoted by one Gulf track two group has been the subject of official deliberations within the GCC and the Arab League.

That said, the filtering of track two concepts has by and large failed to penetrate significant groups outside the dialogue process. Domestic environments make participants cautious about exposing track two ideas to wider audiences. Cooperation with Israel is still a dangerous position in the region, and Israelis are suspicious of cooperative postures that may signal weakness. The regional context of a deadlocked Middle East peace process and the bloody and uncertain aftermath of the Iraq war—not to mention enduring rivalries and power imbalances—make regional discussions of confidence-building and cooperative security difficult even in the Gulf context. Ideas supporting regional security cooperation are still unknown or unpopular among vast segments of the population throughout the Middle East.

Key South Asia Findings

As in the Middle East, South Asia experienced a growth in track two dialogues in the 1990s, and many of these efforts continue today. While unofficial dialogues initially focused more on regional economic and development issues, they have become increasingly political, with several focusing explicitly on core political and security issues such as nuclear proliferation and the status of Kashmir.

The direct impact of South Asian dialogues on official policy has been limited, although not entirely absent. For example, one track two group promoted the idea of a joint pipeline to pump natural gas from Iran to India and Pakistan—addressing the growing energy needs of the two countries while also serving as a peace-building exercise. With the renewal of the Indian-Pakistani peace process, the pipeline idea moved to the official track. In another instance, a prominent Pakistani general who was involved in a variety of track two dialogues and published a book supportive of cooperative security concepts is now serving as the Pakistani ambassador to the United States, improving the prospects for track two ideas to filter into official thinking.

A number of confidence-building measures (CBMs) initially discussed in track two forums are now being officially implemented between India and Pakistan, such as the ballistic missile flight test notification agreement, military exercise notifications and constraint measures along international borders, and Kashmir-related CBMs. Similarly, ideas based on track two workshops promoting nuclear risk reduction measures have now surfaced as part of the official Indian-Pakistani dialogue.

South Asian dialogues have also succeeded in changing mind-sets among participants toward more cooperative postures and have had some success in building a constituency supportive of South Asian cooperation, including in challenging areas such as nuclear confidence-building and new approaches to Kashmir. In one case, Indian policy-makers who had attended track two workshops repackaged ideas proposed by extraregionals into their own initiative calling for an organization to monitor the implementation of Indian-Pakistani CBMs.

Filtering is also apparent from the emergence of a variety of regional policy centers focused on issues that are being discussed in track two venues. The growth of indigenous institutions, centers, and dialogues has fostered a sense of regional ownership and identity and has provided legitimacy to track two groups. Local and regional policy centers also broaden the scope and nature of track two participants to involve wider segments of society, including women and youth.

Despite such progress, South Asian dialogues also face challenges. Some elites involved in track two dialogues are still attached to national positions and resist change. More open-minded participants may have difficulty penetrating well-established thinking in official government circles. Government officials are often suspicious of track two processes, and there are no established mechanisms for transferring track two ideas to officials beyond informal and ad hoc contacts.

The continued mistrust of the adversary also makes cooperative security ideas a difficult sell. India has traditionally preferred to deal with its neighbors bilaterally (where its dominance is assured) rather than multilaterally. The prevailing strategic mind-set fosters zero-sum thinking and creates an aversion to CBMs. Indeed, there is regionwide suspicion of CBMs as a foreign import.

Domestic institutions in both India and Pakistan, particularly their intelligence services, are similarly hostile to CBMs that require more transparency in military budgets and defense doctrines. Until security and foreign policy institutions within India, particularly the military, view cooperative security as a benefit rather than a costly imposition, it will be difficult for track two forums to make progress. Finally, the asymmetric relationship between India and its neighbors and the regional conflicts along India's borders, particularly the ongoing dispute with Pakistan over control of Kashmir, create a violent regional environment that is not conducive to regional cooperation.

Regional Comparisons

The case chapters (Chapters Two and Three) underscore the ways in which the Middle East and South Asia face similarly hostile environments for cooperative security ideas and activities promoted through track two efforts. Neither in the Middle East nor in South Asia is there a common perception of external or internal threats that might propel regional actors toward greater regional cooperation; instead, threat perceptions are often based on actors from within the region or even from within respective societies.

Moreover, both the Middle East and South Asia are dominated by security elites with realist mind-sets, and competitive and zero-sum thinking is pervasive. Cooperative security is a difficult concept in regions where the conventional wisdom is that nuclear weapons are vital for security and where the risks associated with such weapons are not widely understood or acknowledged.

The most powerful actors in both regions—Israel and India—do not view arms control as a vital national interest, nor are they inclined to support regional multilateral security forums, preferring instead bilateral security arrangements with regional neighbors and external actors. Both India and Israel have a similar approach to the sequencing of cooperative security and arms control, with each preferring to first pursue broad agendas of CBMs that address a range of regional issues before focusing on the core issues that their adversaries seek to highlight (nuclear weapons and the Palestinian track in the case of Israel; Kashmir in the case of India).

Still, track two groups in both regions have made considerable progress in socialization. Thousands of military and civilian elites have discussed and engaged in cooperative security exercises. Expertise and knowledge of basic arms control concepts were limited in both regions before the 1990s. Now, because of track two dialogues, there are large communities of well-connected individuals familiar with such concepts. Knowledge of complex arms control and regional security concepts and operational confidence-building activity is now solidly rooted in both regions.

The South Asian track two experience appears to have gone further than that of the Middle East. The public in South Asia is generally more supportive of reconciliation, particularly because recognition of key regional actors and diplomatic relations is the norm, unlike the situation in the Middle East, where normalization with Israel is still taboo among many governments and the majority of people in the region. South Asians are also culturally similar, allowing for greater potential for the development of peace constituencies at the grassroots level. Such similarities are missing in the Arab-Israeli context (of course, inter-Arab dialogues do not face this problem, but the gap between Arabs and Iranians is significant). In the Middle East, Arab governments are ahead of the public in terms of reconciliation with Israel; in South Asia, the reverse appears to be the case.

Perhaps in part because South Asia's public is more receptive to reconciliation efforts, track two ideas are spreading to more societal groups in the region and leading to the development of more cooperative regional centers. These developments could also be linked to the stronger tradition of democracy in South Asia. Open discussion of the nuclear issue in South Asia since the 1998 nuclear tests has further facilitated filtering, as advocacy groups focusing on the issue have developed. In contrast, societal nuclear activism is still absent in the Middle East.

Regional Lessons

The more advanced stage and effect of unofficial dialogues in South Asia, as well as the fact that it is now an openly nuclear region, offer lessons and predictions for the Middle East. On the nuclear front, many analysts are concerned that the Indian-Pakistani nuclear relationship will not follow the stability of the U.S.-Soviet deterrence model and that the potential for miscalculation and accidents could lead to catastrophic results. Of particular concern is the safety of Pakistan's nuclear arsenal given the domestic instability in that country and the lack of civilian control over the military. An additional worry is that Pakistan's technology could spread to rogue state actors or nonstate terrorist groups seeking nuclear options (following the example of Abdul Qadeer Khan, the Pakistani scientist who sold nuclear technology to Iran, Libya, and North Korea). The growing military disparity between India and Pakistan could also be a source of future instability, leading to scenarios that suggest more aggressive Indian behavior.

Such concerns are likely to be replicated and viewed with even more alarm in the Middle East if Iran acquires nuclear capability. This is particularly the case given that nuclear breakout is unlikely to remain limited to a bipolar relationship between Israel and Iran but, rather, is more likely to lead to a multipolar nuclear region. As in the case of South Asia, many analysts worry that the Cold War model of nuclear stability will not hold. Indeed, the multipolar nature of a future nuclear Middle East could prove even more destabilizing than the current situation in South Asia, where at least the nuclear issue is contained to two central adversaries.

Still, the nuclear restraint regime that has been developing between India and Pakistan—with many of its components developed in track two dialogues—offers concrete examples for the Middle East. Ideas focused on creating a nuclear safe zone in South Asia—as opposed to a more ambitious nuclear free zone—will be an especially important experiment that Middle Easterners will want to track closely.

While the South Asian nuclear experience raises important lessons for actors in the Middle East, the more immediate impact of the 1998 nuclear tests has been on the conventional front. The potential for nuclear weapons to lead to greater aggressiveness and conflict on the conventional battlefield has played out in South Asia and offers a cautionary message for future Middle East security relationships. Such dangers underscore the need to utilize track two security dialogues to create and improve channels of communication among regional adversaries and lay the groundwork for conceptual and operational CBMs that will help prevent, or at least contain, future conflicts.

Acknowledgments

I am indebted to many individuals who helped bring this project to completion. First and foremost is the support from the Smith Richardson Foundation and its senior program officer, Allan Song, who initially sponsored and funded this research through a junior faculty grant when I was an assistant professor at George Washington University (GW). I also wish to thank Edward McCord for helping administer the grant at GW and securing Elliott School support for the work.

I am also grateful to Jan Melissen for housing me as a visiting fellow at the Netherlands Institute of International Relations (Clingendael) in the spring of 2005 to work on the project and for sponsoring part of my earlier work as a Clingendael diplomacy paper. At RAND, I owe many thanks to Rachel M. Swanger and James Dobbins for reading the entire manuscript and moving it forward toward publication. I also would like to acknowledge the assistance of other RAND colleagues, particularly Gene Gritton, Michael Lostumbo, Nurith Berstein, Josh Levine, James Torr, Ron Miller, Stephen Bloodsworth, and John Warren. The capable administrative assistance of Isabel Sardou and, especially, Terri Perkins at RAND helped in the preparation of the monograph during the final stages of the process.

I owe a special thanks to Michael Yaffe for serving as an external reviewer and for providing helpful comments, information, and insights throughout the process, and indeed even before the monograph was fully formed. I would also like to acknowledge the generous assistance of Peter Jones, who read an earlier version of the manuscript and provided extremely useful feedback, particularly on the Middle East sections.

I am also grateful to David Griffiths for sharing his knowledge concerning maritime track two efforts in both the Middle East and South Asia and to Steven Spiegel for his general insights on track two in the Middle East. Gary Sick and Michael Kraig also helped me understand various Gulf processes, and Lana Nusseibeh provided helpful information on the Gulf Research Center's efforts. On South Asia, I wish to thank Teresita Schaffer and Robert Einhorn at the Center for Strategic and International Studies for sharing their expertise and insights, and I would also like to thank Michael Krepon at the Stimson Center.

There are also dozens of extraregional and regional participants and organizers—official and unofficial—whose names I cannot list here who generously gave of their time to discuss their impressions and knowledge of track two in both regions. I am deeply grateful to every one of these individuals; indeed, this monograph would not have been possible without their assistance.

Abbreviations

ACRS	Arms Control and Regional Security Working Group
ARF	ASEAN Regional Forum
ASEAN	Association of Southeast Asian Nations
CBM	confidence-building measure
CCW	Convention on Certain Conventional Weapons
CFPS	Centre for Foreign Policy Studies
CMC	Cooperative Monitoring Center
CRC	Chemical Risks Consortium
CSBM	confidence- and security-building measure
CSCAP	Council for Security Cooperation in the Asia Pacific
CSIS	Center for Strategic and International Studies
CTBT	Comprehensive Test Ban Treaty
CWC	Chemical Weapons Convention
DoD	U.S. Department of Defense
EuroMeSCo	Euro-Mediterranean Study Commission
GCC	Gulf Cooperation Council

GRC	Gulf Research Council
GWMDFZ	Gulf Weapons of Mass Destruction Free Zone
IGCC	Institute on Global Conflict and Cooperation
IISS	International Institute for Strategic Studies
INCSEA	incident at sea
INEGMA	Institute for Near East and Gulf Military Analysis
KSG	Kashmir Study Group
LOC	Line of Control
MarSaf	Maritime Safety Colloquium
MECIDS	Middle East Consortium of Infectious Disease Surveillance
MIMA	Maritime Institute of Malaysia
NESA	Near East South Asia Center for Strategic Studies
NGO	nongovernmental organization
NPT	Nuclear Non-Proliferation Treaty
NRRC	nuclear risk reduction centre
OSCE	Organization for Security and Co-Operation in Europe
PLO	Palestine Liberation Organization
RCSS	Regional Centre for Strategic Studies
SAARC	South Asian Association for Regional Cooperation
SAR	search and rescue
SEANWFZ	Southeast Asia Nuclear Weapon–Free Zone
SIPRI	Stockholm International Peace Research Institute

UCLA	University of California, Los Angeles
UNESCO	United Nations Educational, Scientific, and Cultural Organisation
UNIDIR	United Nations Institute for Disarmament Research
VERTIC	Verification Research Training and Information Centre
WMD	weapons of mass destruction
WMDFZ	weapons of mass destruction free zone

CHAPTER ONE

Rethinking Track Two Diplomacy

Key Issues and Questions

How do adversaries manage to sit down and talk about long-standing conflicts while violence and mistrust continue to define their security relations?[1] While official diplomatic communications are the obvious way for adversaries to talk, in many instances adversaries cannot communicate openly given domestic sensitivities, particularly in cases in which parties may lack diplomatic relations or even officially deny the existence of the other. Because of such limitations, adversaries have often turned to unofficial channels, a method known as track two diplomacy. Although track two dialogues have taken place in a variety of conflict-prone regions for decades, they have significantly increased in popularity since the end of the Cold War. Foundations, nongovernmental organizations (NGOs), universities, and governments—mostly based in the West—have devoted significant financial and human resources to such dialogues. What has been the payoff?

This study examines track two efforts in two particularly conflict-prone regions: the Middle East and South Asia. Hundreds of unofficial regional security-related[2] dialogues have taken place across these

---

[1] Sections of this chapter draw on Kaye (2005, 2001b).

[2] This study assumes a broad definition of security, extending beyond military and strategic issues to areas such as economic development, water, the environment, and social reform. While many regional security dialogues focus on regional arms control, the notion of cooperative security—which many of these dialogues advance—implies the need to view security more comprehensively. On cooperative security concepts, see Nolan (1994).

regions—involving academics, diplomats, policy analysts, NGO activists, journalists, and parliamentarians—for over 15 years. Because of the long-standing nature of the conflict and the strategic importance of the Middle East and South Asia to vital security interests in the West, these regions pose significant challenges for efforts to improve relations and cooperation among adversaries.

These regions also provide useful cases to assess the nature and influence of track two dialogues by raising several critical questions: What has been the impact of such dialogues? Do we see similar types of track two efforts in these regions? Can we discern similar patterns of influence on regional security thinking and policy? Do the cases illustrate common impediments to track two efforts in non-Western contexts? If similar external actors have applied track two efforts in comparable ways, how might we explain differences in results across the two regions? Can differences between the cases suggest conditions under which track two efforts are more or less likely to succeed? What lessons can both regions suggest for other cases?

The State of the Field

Despite the growth of track two activities, there has been scant analysis of the nature and effectiveness of regional security track two dialogues, and a limited number of studies comparing such processes in different regional contexts. Most of the current literature on track two diplomacy is limited to the conflict resolution field, offering largely positive assessments and overstating the effect of such dialogues.[3]

---

[3] A notable exception is *Track-II Diplomacy: Lessons from the Middle East* (Agha et al., 2003). While this book is primarily concerned with track two's effect on conflict resolution, the analysis suggests both the impact and the limitations of such diplomacy. The book also makes an attempt to assess the effectiveness of track two dialogues, although the bulk of the analysis concerns Arab-Israeli bilateral track two dialogues in which the objective is to influence a track one negotiation. Only one chapter addresses the issue of regional security dialogues, for which the authors acknowledge it is more difficult to assess effectiveness. That said, the fact that the book is the result of Arab-Israeli collaboration (all of the authors participated in track two dialogues) suggests that track two venues have had some success in

Much of this literature emphasizes the psychological dynamics of track two discussions, particularly the claim that such exercises can transform the image of the adversary, or humanize the "other," and thus lead to new relationships conducive to the resolution of deep-seated conflicts.[4] At the other end of the spectrum, one encounters either neglect of such activities in mainstream international relations research or skeptical assessments from policy practitioners who see few if any concrete results from such unofficial endeavors—i.e., break-throughs in regional peace processes or major adjustments in security policy. Missing are more balanced assessments of both the potential and the limits of track two dialogue and a more realistic understanding of its functions.

A Normative Framework

The Middle East and South Asia cases underscore that track two dialogues are primarily about long-term socialization and the generation of new ideas, not immediate policy change. Such dialogues are a conditioning process in which regionals are exposed to new concepts, adapt them to their own contexts, and shape policy debates over time. Thus, the common attempt to associate track two dialogues with tangible outcomes such as the immediate resolution of bilateral conflict—most closely identified with the Israeli-Palestinian Oslo process—needs reas-

---

moving regional thinking toward common understandings and conceptions of key regional problems.

[4] An example of such literature is McDonald and Bendahmane (1987), although this volume also contains contributions which point to several limitations of track two diplomacy, such as Saunders (1987). Other examples include Volkan, Montville, and Julius (1991) and Burton and Dukes (1990). Diamond and McDonald (1991, p. 44) even suggest that "Track Two is extending the peacemaking mode far beyond conflict resolution to the uncharted territory of planetary healing." Davies and Kaufman's (2002) edited volume focuses more on the civil society–building potential of track two diplomacy than on its psychological effect on participants, but like previous works it also provides a generally optimistic account of such activities and places them squarely in the peace-building realm.

sessment.[5] Unlike the Oslo model, many regional track two dialogues are not necessarily intended to have an immediate influence on track one negotiations.[6]

Instead, many unofficial dialogues are either bilateral or multilateral attempts to address or define regional security problems. The goal of such efforts is usually not formal conflict resolution through contributions to a peace settlement, but rather conflict management, tension reduction, confidence building, and the formation of regional or subregional identities that allow actors to frame and approach problems in similar ways. This is especially the case in security-related dialogues, which are often regionally based and, in the cases of the Middle East and South Asia, largely seek to create a cooperative regional security framework.

Such an understanding of track two dialogues speaks to growing political science research that emphasizes the role of norms and ideas in shaping interests and identity, as well as more recent work on socialization.[7] While a large body of this literature focuses on the role of international organizations and nongovernmental actors in shaping the normative context for international relations and state behavior,[8] scholars focusing on socialization and communication have observed

---

[5] For an analysis of the negotiating process at Oslo, see Pruitt (1997). For the larger political context leading up to Oslo, see Makovsky (1996).

[6] Rouhana (1999) makes a similar observation regarding the role of unofficial dialogues, although he uses the term *unofficial intervention* to characterize the problem-solving workshops sponsored by third parties to address ethnic and national conflicts. Other analysts, notably Harold Saunders, also view such dialogues as part of a long-term conflict resolution process (Saunders, 1987). In his more recent work on "circum-negotiation," Saunders (1996) argues that unofficial policy dialogues (or "public dialogues") are an important component in reshaping the larger political environment in efforts to move peace processes among conflicting parties forward.

[7] The "constructivist" school in international relations is most closely associated with such research. On constructivism, see Wendt (1999), Katzenstein (1996), and Checkel (1998). On socialization in international politics, see Ikenberry and Kupchan (1990), Johnston (2001), Acharya (2004a), Adler (1992), and Checkel (2001). For an extensive discussion of socialization through European institutions, see *International Organization*, 2005.

[8] See, for example, Finnemore (1996), Finnemore and Sikkink (1998), Keck and Sikkink (1998), Risse, Ropp, and Sikkink (1999), and Klotz (1995).

that normative influence can occur not only in the public sphere but also through diplomatic channels.[9] Indeed, diplomacy is not just about producing negotiated outcomes but also about influencing how others think.[10] Actors involved in negotiations are not always negotiating agreements based on fixed preferences: They are also involved in an ongoing dialogue that may shape and even change preferences based on new normative beliefs. This is even more evident in track two diplomacy, which is almost entirely about influencing thinking and conceptions of interests as opposed to negotiating formal treaties.

Defining Track Two

To identify the types of activities examined in this study, it is necessary to define what we mean by "track two." The broadest definition of *track two diplomacy* refers to interactions among individuals or groups that take place outside an official negotiation process. Thus, while "track one" refers to all official, governmental diplomacy (bilateral or multilateral), track two describes all other activities that occur outside official government channels.[11] As Louise Diamond and John McDonald explain, track two refers to "non-governmental, informal and unofficial contacts and activities between private citizens or groups of individuals, sometimes called 'non-state actors'" (1991, p. 1). McDonald offers a similar definition, suggesting that track two is informal and unofficial "interaction between private citizens or groups of people within a country or from different countries who are outside the formal governmen-

---

[9] See, for example, Risse (2000). For a different and more political, power-based view of arguing, see Crawford (2002).

[10] For a view of diplomacy as representing and shaping identities rather than negotiating fixed outcomes, see Sharp (1999).

[11] Joe Montville first used the term *track two diplomacy* in Davidson and Montville (1981–1982). Although the term did not enter common usage until the mid-1980s, similar ideas and practices had been discussed long before, particularly in the conflict resolution community of scholars and practitioners. For example, Nathan Funk (2000, p. 26) cites several studies that have drawn on similar concepts (e.g., citizen diplomacy, public diplomacy, unofficial diplomacy, nonofficial mediation, and analytic problem solving).

tal power structure" (McDonald and Bendahmane, 1987, p. 1). However, these types of definitions are so broad that any nongovernmental activity could constitute track two, including business contacts, citizen exchange programs, advocacy work, or religious contacts.[12]

In contrast, this study focuses on a subset of unofficial activity that involves professional contacts among elites from adversarial groups with the purpose of addressing policy problems in efforts to analyze, prevent, manage, and ultimately resolve intergroup or interstate conflicts. As Harold Saunders suggests, track two diplomacy involves citizens who engage in "policy-related, problem-solving dialogue" in which they may discuss "elements of the overall political relationship, solutions to arms control problems, resolution of regional conflicts, issues of trade policy, or other areas of competition" (1991, p. 49). Saunders distinguishes this type of interaction from "people-to-people" diplomacy, in which the objective is solely "getting to know the other side" and developing personal experiences with one's adversaries (such as student exchanges) rather than finding solutions to problems (1991, p. 50).[13] For the purposes of this study, track two diplomacy relates to policy and involves consciously organized problem-solving exercises.[14]

That said, such dialogues—particularly in the regional security area—are not necessarily "hard" track two exercises in which the objective is to help governments negotiate political agreements. For example, many analysts and practitioners associate track two dialogues with the most notable case in the Middle East, the Israeli-Palestinian track two talks in Oslo in the early 1990s. The Oslo model, which led directly to a formal peace process between Israel and the Palestine Liberation Organization (PLO), suggests secret, back-channel, bilateral talks with the specific objective of resolving a conflict between two adversaries. While this is certainly an important model for conflict resolution, it is not the only model. Indeed, most regional security dialogues are engaged via "soft" track two discussions, which "are aimed at an exchange of

---

[12] Indeed, Diamond and McDonald (1991) refer to these types of activities (and others) as distinct types of diplomacy, breaking down the concept into nine tracks.

[13] Also see Rouhana (1999).

[14] These distinctions are based on Kelman (1991).

views, perceptions, and information among the parties to improve each side's understanding of the other's positions and policies" (Agha et al., 2003).[15] However, even "soft" track two exchanges are policy-related and ultimately aim to address and solve key security challenges.[16]

Moreover, track two participants are expected to have some communication with government policymakers (many participants are often influential former government officials, active or retired military personnel, think-tank specialists, and journalists) so that the ideas discussed in the unofficial setting have the prospect both to reflect and to filter into the thinking of official policy circles. Many of the participants are also officials participating in a private capacity. Because the participants have considerable access to the official policy process, such a conception of track two dialogues resembles what some call "track one and a half."[17]

Unlike track two processes in other regions (such as Southeast Asia), neither the Middle East nor South Asia has formal institutional channels through which government officials can be briefed on track two activities. Rather, such communications usually take place informally, as unofficial elites either brief relevant officials through personal connections or write opinion pieces and articles reflecting the thinking that emerges from such discussions. Official participants attending in an unofficial capacity can directly transfer information they have acquired through track two activities to appropriate governmental channels. Unofficial participants in track two dialogues may also later assume official government positions and have the ability to draw on their track two experiences to influence official policy. It is also important to note that track two dialogues are nonbinding, operate under

---

[15] For this distinction between "hard" and "soft" track two diplomacy, see Agha et al. (2003).

[16] In this way, regional track two dialogues more closely resemble Saunders's circumnegotiation concept than a more formal prenegotiation process because they are contributing to changing the overall political environment in which peace processes operate rather than serving as forums to prepare the groundwork for specific negotiations and treaties. On this distinction, see Saunders (1996). On prenegotiation, see Stein (1989).

[17] For an elaboration of this term, see Smock (1998).

Chatham House rules,[18] offer voluntary participation, and are generally conducted by NGOs: These attributes ensure that track two dialogues remain unofficial even if governments may at times sanction and fund various initiatives and send officials to participate in unofficial capacities.[19]

This monograph thus defines track two as *unofficial policy dialogue, focused on problem solving, in which the participants have some form of access to official policymaking circles.* While such dialogues can take place bilaterally or multilaterally and focus on a variety of policy issues, the analysis here focuses on *regional* dialogues addressing *security-related* issues. Because peace and stability in the Middle East and South Asia cannot be accomplished without a regional framework that addresses core security threats and perceptions, it is critical to comprehensively examine those processes that consider such issues. This monograph also primarily highlights serial dialogues because such dialogues demonstrate a more serious investment than do one-off meetings and better allow for an examination of effects over time. Consequently, the empirical examination in this monograph is chiefly limited to ongoing regional, multilateral track two security dialogues in the Middle East and South Asia.

Applying Track Two

According to a prominent Southeast Asian analyst, track two dialogues "have shown a remarkable ability to refine and tailor concepts and ideas to suit the local security environment" and "have served as 'filtering mechanisms' for approaches to regional security cooperation developed

---

[18] The nonattribution and off-the-record Chatham House rules that characterize nearly all track two dialogues make such processes difficult to penetrate for outside researchers. This may help explain the lack of comprehensive research on this topic and the need to have access to a large number of participants to build an accurate picture of the dynamics of such processes. While this study benefited from considerable access to track two participants and organizers, the at times incomplete information about particular groups is largely a result of this constraint.

[19] I thank Michael Yaffe for bringing these additional attributes to my attention.

in other parts of the world" (Acharya, 1998, p. 76). Does the same dynamic apply in the Middle East and South Asia? To what extent do track two dialogues in these regions serve as "socialization" and "filtering" processes whereby extraregional—usually Western—concepts and norms are discussed in a regional context and potentially become localized and adapted to a regional environment?[20]

Indeed, most security-related track two dialogues in the Middle East and South Asia begin by studying extraregional concepts and models related to cooperative security in order to stimulate ideas about how to move regional thinking away from traditional *realpolitik* into more cooperative postures.[21] If filtering at the regional level proves successful, track two dialogues can legitimize such ideas and improve the prospects for cooperative security concepts to influence official policy circles and the wider public over time. Both cases will assess the extent to which such normative influence has taken place, and the factors that might impede such influence.

To make such assessments, Chapters Two and Three review the most significant regional security dialogues in each region. Each chapter then addresses the extent to which, in practice, such efforts lend support to the conceptual stages I identify as defining the evolution of track two dialogues: socialization, filtering, and policy adjustment.

Evidence for socialization is based on changed perceptions among participating elites, based on interview data and written material from participants; project organizers may also look for specific measures of success during this stage that focus on the progress of the dialogue group itself, such as the ability to secure funding, the frequency of meetings, or publications reflecting collaboration among former adver-

---

[20] On filtering, see Acharya (1998).

[21] That said, although the focus on cooperative security rather than *realpolitik* is common in many dialogues promoted by the West, it is not inherent in any track two discussion. For example, in the case of U.S.-Japan dialogues, the focus has been on moving the Japanese *toward* rather than away from realist postures. Thus, the content of track two dialogues and their socialization function is not by definition cooperative in content. I thank Rachel M. Swanger for this observation.

saries.[22] Indicators for filtering include examples of new regional security institutes or organizations and evidence that track two ideas have reached segments of society outside of the track two dialogue group. Policy adjustment would be suggested by examples of concrete changes in various areas of security policy, such as military doctrines or new political agreements.

To the extent that track two dialogues have not managed to fulfill these functions in either region, the case chapters (Chapters Two and Three) examine a similar set of impediments at three levels of analysis: the nature of participating elites, domestic constraints, and the state of the larger regional environment. Chapter Four assesses and compares the cases and provides lessons for improving these and other dialogues in the future.

A Regional Focus

The previous discussion suggested that security-related dialogues are designed more to create a regional context to address and discuss important security issues than to resolve immediate bilateral disputes. In this sense, we might view regional dialogues—especially multilateral security forums—as "region-building" efforts to establish regional norms and institutions.[23]

Academic research is increasingly turning to regions as an important level of analysis at which to examine interstate and transnational interactions.[24] Security dynamics differ across various regions, while the impact of globalization plays out differently across different areas of

---

[22] Thanks to Michael Yaffe for suggesting these measures of effectiveness as ways for project organizers to evaluate the impact of their efforts.

[23] Reference to this specific term can be found in Neumann (1994), although more recent policy-oriented studies have also drawn on this concept. See, for example, Ortega (2004, pp. 117–128).

[24] For examples, see Buzan and Waever (2003), Lemke (2002), Lake and Morgan (1997), Fawcett and Hurrell (1995), Solingen (1998), Adler and Barnett (1998), and Kaye (unpublished manuscript).

the world.[25] Whether scholars are focusing on material interdependencies and externalities or on the development of regional identities and security communities where a common "we feeling" prevails, international relations research is recognizing the importance of examining regional dynamics.

Policy-oriented analysts are also increasingly focused on regions, with some arguing that regional cooperation can provide a source of stability and conflict prevention.[26] The ongoing conflicts in Afghanistan and Iraq have underscored the importance of a regional approach to address the complexities of such challenges, as extraregional actors cannot resolve such conflicts without the engagement of key regional neighbors.[27] Others suggest that with the inevitable decline of American hegemony, more attention should be paid to regional solutions for world order (Kupchan, 1998). Some argue that a cooperative regional security environment can assist the internal process of political reform within nations located in volatile areas (Asmus et al., 2005). Indeed, in terms of the central security dilemmas facing regions such as the Middle East and South Asia, regional cooperative security structures may prove more effective in addressing such challenges than existing global structures given both regions' sensitivity to outside influence and pressure.

Moreover, the view that improved regional cooperation can also improve regional economic development by increasing global investment—a perception shared by policy elites in both the Middle East and South Asia since the 1990s—also suggests the prescriptive value of improving and supporting multilateral regional cooperation. Viewing regions in this way suggests that track two regional security dialogues may be critically important venues to begin the discussion of reshaping regional security relations and establishing or improving existing regional security structures in both the Middle East and South Asia.

---

[25] See Buzan and Waever (2003, especially p. 13) on this point.

[26] See, for example, Acharya (2004b).

[27] The Iraq Study Group, for example, has highlighted the importance of the regional dimension in defusing violence in Iraq (Baker and Hamilton, 2006).

Historical Precedents

The idea of using track two dialogues to promote security cooperation and address long-standing conflicts did not suddenly emerge following the end of the Cold War, although it was at this time that the application of such ideas became more politically feasible in regions such as the Middle East and South Asia. The most important precedent for track two dialogues grew out of the postwar European experience, particularly the U.S.-Soviet context. Numerous East-West arms control dialogues introduced notions of "cooperative" and "mutual" security, concepts that formed the core of subsequent security socialization efforts in other regions (Krause and Latham, 1998). As analysts of such processes explain, "Perhaps the most important legacy of the East-West CSBM [confidence- and security-building measure] experience was a modification of the Western *realpolitik* tradition . . . as a result of the process of negotiating a range of CSBMs with the Soviet Union, the Western policy-community came to believe that security is 'mutual'" (Krause and Latham, 1998, p. 33).

This radical shift in security thinking and the creation of an unprecedented arms control experience began with unofficial dialogues among groups of experts. Such dialogues created an "epistemic community" of arms controllers (Adler, 1992) who were able to reach a broader political audience (bureaucracies, parliaments, interest groups) supportive of cooperative security concepts (Krause and Latham, 1998, p. 45). Leaderships on both sides found such concepts politically useful and desirable and thus co-opted the agenda for their own needs, leading to the formation of arms control regimes and, arguably, the end of U.S.–Soviet conflict. Some have suggested that track two U.S.-Soviet dialogues, such as the so-called Dartmouth talks, created new concepts (such as "complex interdependence" and "common security") that, because of regular Soviet participation, eventually became part of Gorbachev's "new thinking."[28]

---

[28] For details related to the Dartmouth talks, see Stewart (1997). On the impact of the Dartmouth process, see Saunders (1991, particularly p. 66) on the Gorbachev point.

Other analysts have claimed that unofficial transnational movements of scientists and academics as developed through dialogues such as the Pugwash Conference played a role in influencing Soviet ideas and ultimately ending the Cold War.[29] Whether or not one believes that such dialogues led to the end of the Cold War, they did provide a strong foundation for future track two efforts by demonstrating the potential of unofficial contacts to create new concepts and relationships that can, over time and in a ripe political environment, significantly shift security thinking and practice among long-standing adversaries. Of course, the application of such tools to regions such as the Middle East and South Asia is not always appropriate given differences in historical and cultural contexts, a problem that the case chapters highlight. Still, despite such differences, the form and content of many track two exercises today—particularly the menu of confidence-building measures on the table—largely mirror these earlier European and U.S.-Soviet efforts.

Another regional model that has gained attention is the Association of Southeast Asian Nations (ASEAN) and its more recent, related forum, the ASEAN Regional Forum (ARF).[30] Some analysts suggest that ASEAN might provide a better model for security cooperation in non-Western regions than the European experience of highly institutionalized regional cooperation (see, for example, McMillan, Sokolsky, and Winner, 2003). Indeed, some aspects of ASEAN, particularly its emphasis on personal contacts, informality, and consensus-building rather than formal institutionalized decisionmaking (Acharya, 1998), provide important lessons for the Middle East and South Asia.

---

[29] See Evengelista (1999). For a general overview of the origins and objectives of Pugwash, see the "About" portion of the Pugwash Online Web site (as of June 26, 2007): http://www.pugwash.org/about.htm

[30] ARF, established in 1994, expanded ASEAN's agenda to the security realm (and widened its membership to the larger Asia-Pacific region) as it introduced Western strategic concepts such as confidence-building measures (CBMs), deterrence, arms control, transparency, and verification into regional discussions. Some analysts suggest that track two activity related to ASEAN supported the creation of ARF and the idea of a multilateral regional security structure. See, for example, Rüland (2002).

The popularity of the term *ASEAN way* suggests a degree of independence in establishing cooperative mechanisms that are viewed as legitimate within the region rather than externally imposed. The formation of the ARF also suggests a model for indigenous development of regional institutions.[31] While the ARF is far from a perfect forum for regional security cooperation, the idea of creating a regional forum free from the stigma of outside intervention provides important lessons for attempts to create enduring regional cooperative structures in other areas that are also sensitive to the application of overtly Western concepts. The structured track two regional process sanctioned by ARF, the Council for Security Cooperation in the Asia Pacific (CSCAP), also provides an interesting model for organizing unofficial activity that can feed regional confidence-building and security cooperation ideas and activities into official regional institutions and discussions.[32] Indeed, the decentralized and uneven nature of track two activities in the Middle East and South Asia suggests to some that a better-organized track two umbrella organization may prove more effective in getting track two ideas across to the official level.

That said, in the Middle East case, there is no regional security institution into which one could feed track two ideas, and South Asia's regional institution (the South Asian Association for Regional Cooperation, or SAARC) tends to avoid contentious security issues. Still,

---

[31] Externally generated proposals for creating a regional security structure in Southeast Asia, based on models such as the Organization for Security and Co-Operation in Europe (OSCE), were rejected. Regional actors perceived such models as too Western and institutionalized and proposed the ARF concept instead. See Acharya (1998).

[32] CSCAP was formally established at a meeting in Kuala Lumpur on June 8, 1993, as a nongovernmental track two process for dialogue on security issues in the Asia-Pacific. The original full members came from 10 countries in the Asia-Pacific region: Australia, Canada, Indonesia, Japan, South Korea, Malaysia, the Philippines, Singapore, Thailand, and the United States. More recent members include representatives from New Zealand, Russia, North Korea, Mongolia, the European Union, China, India, Vietnam, Cambodia, and Papua New Guinea. Working groups have addressed a variety of regional security issues in the following areas: comprehensive and cooperative security; CSBMs; maritime cooperation in the North Pacific; and transnational crime. For further details, including the CSCAP charter, see its Web site (as of June 26, 2007): http://www.cscap.org

even without strong regional security institutions, there may be some value to better organizing the wide array of regional security track two activity to maximize influence. However, there are other differences between Southeast Asia's experience and that of either the Middle East or South Asia that may make the transferring of the ASEAN/ARF model difficult.

The economic basis underpinning ASEAN's creation is lacking in both the Middle East and South Asia, where intraregional trade is still minimal. Although Southeast Asia also faces territorial disputes and ethnic and religious strife, the intensity and tractability of such divisions differs from that in either the Middle East or South Asia. And perhaps most critically, the security environment in Southeast Asia is different in that all 10 ASEAN nations have acceded to a Southeast Asia Nuclear Weapon–Free Zone (SEANWFZ), established in 1995 at an ASEAN summit in Bangkok.

With India's and Pakistan's nuclear weapon programs out in the open since the 1998 tests and Israel's widely acknowledged nuclear capabilities (despite its formal policy of nuclear ambiguity), neither region appears close to a nuclear weapon free zone agreement. In fact, ongoing negotiations to prevent Iran from furthering its nuclear capability suggest that the Middle East may be moving in the opposite direction. In this sense, one could argue that the security environment and security dilemmas in the Middle East and South Asia are far more similar to each other than to those of Southeast Asia.

Despite the limits of other regional models, many Western advocates of track two diplomacy view these precedents as underscoring the effectiveness of track two dialogues in addressing seemingly intractable conflicts and transforming security relations among former adversaries. It is thus no coincidence that Western institutions and governments have since drawn on these experiences to promote track two discussions in troubled regions such as the Middle East and South Asia.

Comparing the Middle East and South Asia

The application of track two diplomacy to the Middle East and South Asia poses interesting questions and useful cases for comparison because they share a number of conflict characteristics and regional security challenges. Both regions have experienced similar types of track two security dialogues since the early 1990s, activities that in each case were largely initiated from outside the region.[33]

One of the most apparent commonalities between the regions is that both involve parties disputing territory and sovereignty—with religious and nationalistic undertones—in competitive and dangerous security environments. The dominating bilateral disputes (the Indian-Pakistani dispute over Kashmir and the Israeli-Palestinian conflict over the West Bank and Gaza) overshadow other regional security issues and make the discussion of a broader regional security agenda more difficult. As a result of such disputes, these regions contain populations that mistrust the intentions of their adversaries and produce extremist groups opposed to political compromise.

Terrorism is a constant threat and source of disruption to peace processes in both cases, leading to hardened positions and a reduced willingness to engage and compromise. Despite lengthy peace processes to resolve the core issues of their conflicts, neither region has yet succeeded in resolving such disputes. To make matters worse, both regions include nuclear powers and face a weapon-proliferation problem and a competitive–arms racing environment, with offensive military postures and high defense budgets. Common regional challenges beyond the military realm, such as multiple water disputes, economic underdevelopment, and refugee crises, also threaten regional stability.

Moreover, concern about conflict is not hypothetical: These regions have engaged in numerous wars over the past half-century and remain in a volatile state today. Both regions also include politically unstable and vulnerable regimes, making cooperation and conciliatory actions more difficult. Seemingly mundane logistical problems in orga-

---

[33] The external initiative for such efforts contrasts to that of subregions such as the Asia Pacific, where regional parties have initiated multilateral regional dialogues, particularly Japan. (Interview with Mike Mochizuki, Washington, D.C., December 3, 2001.)

nizing regional dialogues, such as obtaining visas and reasonable airline connections, also pose real barriers to cooperation. Furthermore, neither region has communicated well the existence and nature of track two dialogues to the broader public. (South Asian dialogues have made more progress in this area, particularly as the 1998 nuclear tests in India and Pakistan raised public awareness about proliferation and led to the formation of civil-society groups focused on this issue.)

Another area in common is a similar "cultural" barrier to the acceptance of CBMs given the adversarial and zero-sum environment in which cooperation efforts take place.[34] The zero-sum environment that pervades both regions makes the promotion of CBMs difficult, particularly as they are often viewed as a "foreign import" based on the East-West experience during the Cold War (Krepon, 1996). Indeed, mutual suspicion of CBMs that are generated in the West and a low sense of regional ownership are common to the Middle East and South Asia. That said, some analysts question whether a realist-oriented security elite and a zero-sum environment preclude acceptance of CBMs and regional arms control. For example, although India's strategic elite includes individuals who hold realist assumptions or believe that international politics is about exploitation and inequality, there is no reason that a "realist world-view should prevent arms control. It did not do so in the Soviet-U.S. relationship" (Basur, 2001, p. 183). Indeed, India has agreed to a number of CBMs with both Pakistan and China (Basur, 2001). The same assessment can be applied to the Middle East, where the security elite generally subscribe to realist beliefs but are not always adverse to CBMs and arms control, as the experience of the official multilateral Arms Control and Regional Security (ACRS) Working Group in the 1990s suggests.[35] Still, the competitive security environment makes the acceptance of CBMs and regional arms control more difficult in both regions.

---

[34] On the role of culture in helping to define security interests, see Krause (1998).

[35] On ACRS, see Jentleson and Kaye (1998), Kaye (2001a, Chapter 4), Jones (2005a), U.S. Department of State (2001), Fahmy (2001), Feldman (1997), Griffiths (2000), Jentleson (1996), Jones (1997, 2003), Landau (2001, 2006), and Yaffe (1994).

Finally, the dominant powers in each region—India and Israel—have traditionally resisted multilateral regional security forums and have instead preferred bilateral or trilateral forums (in the Middle East case, with U.S. mediation). India's and Israel's reluctance to engage in multilateral forums stems from concerns about smaller parties "ganging up" on the dominant power and the ability of such forums to become a source of outside pressure (see Krepon, 1996, and Rizvi, 1993, p. 154). India and Israel also stand out in their regions in terms of their relative levels of political and economic development, leading to similar asymmetries that make regional cooperation more difficult. Taken together, the significant similarities of the Middle East and South Asian security environments suggest an interesting and appropriate point of comparison.

The similarity between these regions does not suggest, however, that we should ignore their contrasting historical, social, and political contexts. A deeper culture and history of political democracy and liberalism in South Asia than in the Middle East, for example, is an important difference that could potentially influence how well security cooperation filters into regional thinking given the importance of civil-society groups at this stage of track two development. The cultural ties and similarities among South Asian states, including adversaries such as India and Pakistan, also suggest potential for publics to pressure governments toward accommodating positions if a favorable political context emerges. Such cultural similarities and societal pressures are missing in the Arab-Israeli context (or in Arab-Iranian relations), although they are more apparent in the inter-Arab context.

Another apparent difference is the existence in South Asia of a formal regional institution to support regional cooperation, the SAARC.[36] Although this forum has mainly addressed areas of functional cooperation (such as trade, telecommunications, the environment, energy, and water) and has to date avoided sensitive security

---

[36] SAARC was established in 1985 and includes the seven South Asian states: Bangladesh, Bhutan, India, the Maldives, Nepal, Pakistan, and Sri Lanka. Afghanistan joined SAARC in 2005. On SAARC, see Rizvi (1993, especially pp. 147–162). For a critique of SAARC's limited focus on technical issues, see Bhargava, Bongartz, and Sobhan (1995).

issues, the institution nevertheless includes the key parties involved in the central dispute dominating the regional security environment. The existence of such a forum at least allows for the development of a regional security discourse and possibly the expansion of cooperation to traditional security areas. SAARC has also provided a venue for critical bilateral discussions on the sidelines of its meetings, such as the meeting between Indian prime minister Atal Vajpayee and Pakistani president Pervez Musharraf in January 2004 that began the current peace process between the two countries.[37] A regional institution such as SAARC thus provides additional potential for unofficial regional security discussions to filter into official thinking and institutional structures.

In contrast, since the freezing of the official multilateral Arab-Israeli peace process in the late 1990s (which also included groups working on more technical issues such as the environment and water) and the breakdown of its ACRS Working Group in 1995, the Middle East has had no comprehensive regional security forum. More recently, there has been some discussion about reestablishing such a process, particularly at the subregional level, focusing on the Gulf states (see, for example, Kraig, 2004). But without a regionwide forum that addresses a range of regional security issues and perceptions that overlap all subregions, real progress toward regional security cooperation and greater stability will prove difficult.

In summary, the key similarities between the Middle East and South Asian regional security environments are as follows:

- core disputes over territory and sovereignty involving nationalist and religious dimensions
- competitive security environments
- adverse security cultures for CBMs
- dominant bilateral disputes disrupting larger regional agendas
- regions with states possessing nuclear weapon capabilities
- lack of common threat perceptions, external or internal

[37] For background on the current peace initiative and an assessment of its prospects, see United States Institute of Peace (2005).

- deep mistrust of the adversary
- violent extremist groups opposed to political compromise
- terrorism is a constant threat
- experience of multiple regional wars
- vulnerable and politically unstable regimes
- sensitivity to overt Western support
- low intraregional trade and economic cooperation
- logistical barriers to regional cooperation (e.g., visas, borders, airline connections)
- dominant regional powers (Israel and India) opposed to multilateral regional security regimes
- no formal regional institution to support regional track two activities
- track two dialogues boosted by advances in regional peace processes.

The key differences between the security environments in the two regions are as follows:

- stronger culture of democracy in South Asia
- stronger cultural ties between adversaries in South Asia (India and Pakistan) than in the Middle East (Israel and Arab/Muslim states)
- greater domestic opposition to reconciliation with the adversary in the Middle East
- existence of formal regional cooperation institution in South Asia (SAARC) and its absence in the Middle East
- lengthy record of nuclear CBMs in South Asia; no such public record in the Middle East (although tacit understandings between some Middle East states are possible)
- more centers and networks supportive of regional security cooperation in South Asia
- nuclear activism/social movements developing in South Asia; still taboo in the Middle East.

Roles for Track Two Dialogues

This section outlines in more detail the particular roles that track two dialogues can potentially play in shaping regional relations and in the construction of regional security structures. However, it is important to reiterate at the outset that, in practice, few regional dialogues reach the more ambitious goal of changing security perceptions to the point that official policy also changes, leading to the resolution of long-standing conflicts. Most track two security dialogues play more modest roles, largely influencing the thinking of the elites who participate in such discussions and laying the groundwork for long-term policy adjustments. To better understand the scope of regional security dialogues, it is useful to conceptualize their roles as a staged process—although in practice these stages are not necessarily sequential, and feedback from later stages to earlier ones is possible (see Figure 1.1). For the sake of clarity, I divide these stages into three parts:

1. socialization of the participating elites
2. "filtering" of externally generated policy ideas to the local environment
3. transmission to official policy.

Figure 1.1
The Track Two Influence Process

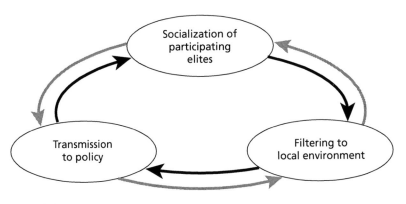

RAND *MG592-1.1*

Socialization of Participating Elites: Creating a Constituency for Regional Cooperation

The initial stages of track two dialogues usually entail a socialization process, whereby outside experts, often from Western governments or nongovernmental institutions, organize forums to share security concepts based on experiences from their own regions with regional actors.[38] This stage is focused primarily on encouraging a small group of influential policy elites to think differently about regional security and the value of regional security cooperation, providing new terms of reference and information about specific security issues. This process also involves frequent interactions among regionals to limit misperceptions and inaccurate assumptions that could undermine progress in formal negotiations.[39] The idea is to target elites who have access to official policymakers and who would, over time, convey such ideas to the official level and to the larger public (through opinion pieces, lectures, interviews, and so on). The assumption of such dialogues is that small groups of well-connected elites specializing in security issues are the essential trigger for broader shifts in official security policy. That said, actual policy change at later stages is unlikely to come without wider domestic support.

First, the most crucial function during the socialization period is education—for example, the development of arms control expertise among a select group of policy elites. In the Middle East and South Asia, regional expertise and knowledge of basic arms control concepts were limited before the 1990s. Now, there are large communities in both regions (including many well-connected individuals) familiar with such concepts because of track two dialogues.

Second, during the socialization process, the regional parties gain a better understanding of mutual threat perceptions. Third, socialization of regional elites involves not only sharing experiences regarding CBMs with regional actors (particularly the U.S.-Soviet and European

---

[38] On this type of socialization, which is based on powerful actors trying to spread their own ideas and norms to others in the international system, see Ikenberry and Kupchan (1990). On the notion of "teaching" norms to international actors, see Finnemore (1996).

[39] I thank Michael Yaffe for raising this point.

experiences), but also engaging the parties in their own CBMs, often in less contentious areas such as maritime cooperation.[40] Fourth, socialization targets not just general security policy elites but also military elites in an attempt to create transnational military dialogues and common understandings. Indeed, some track two dialogues in the Middle East have specifically targeted military elites, and many South Asian dialogues include participants with military backgrounds, albeit usually retired officials whose links to current official policymakers may be tenuous. In both the Middle East and South Asia, military elites play a crucial role in the formation of security policy.[41] In many countries in these regions, it is difficult to separate military from civilian elites at high levels of government, underscoring the need to influence the military community for any future changes in security policy.

Filtering: Making Others' Ideas Your Own

In the typical model of externally initiated track two dialogues in other regional settings, we see that after a period of socialization, regional elites seek to transform such processes into their own and adapt them to the local environment. The ability to translate outside concepts to the local context is critical to the success of track two dialogues; without regional and domestic legitimacy, track two dialogues cannot influence security policy even in the long run.

Thus, this stage involves widening the constituency favoring regional cooperation beyond a select number of policy elites to the larger societal level, through the media, parliament, NGOs, education systems, and citizen interest groups. In practice, this stage has often posed the weak link in track two dialogues, as there has been little translation of the ideas developed in regional security dialogues to groups outside the socialized circle of elites.

The key element in such transmission must be the creation of a discourse that frames issues in ways that show how cooperation can

---

[40] On maritime CBMs in the Middle East, see Griffiths (2000) and Jones (1996).

[41] For a discussion of civil-military relations in the Arab and Islamic worlds, and illustrations of the strong influence of the military on state policy in countries such as Egypt and Pakistan, see Cook (2004).

benefit the interests of participating parties. Essentially, for security policy to shift, long-standing security policies must be reframed in the public debate. For example, a discourse could suggest that regional conflict is not due to the adversary's malign intentions, but instead to each party's perception of its own insecurity, perceptions that are leading to a security dilemma and the potential for accidental war. Conflicts can be framed in a way that shows that cooperation in areas such as arms control can bolster, rather than undermine, a nation's security. The goal at this stage is to use track two dialogues and their participants to spread ideas and create regional structures that transform the notion of regional cooperation into a regional idea serving regional interests, not an extraregional imposition serving the interests of others.

Evidence suggesting filtering includes the creation of new regional institutions or structures supporting cooperative security concepts, joint regional papers proposing new ideas for regional cooperation, discourse on regional security issues at the broader societal level (such as in parliament or the media), and cooperative regional projects initiated by regionals themselves.

Transmission: Turning Ideas into New Policies

The final stage of track two activity is the transmission of the ideas fostered in such dialogues to tangible shifts in security policy, such as altered military or security doctrines, lower defense budgets, or new regional arms control regimes. Neither the Middle East nor South Asia has reached this stage, although ideas discussed in track two settings have contributed to a variety of CBMs currently under way or implemented in the official Indian-Pakistani peace process, even if fundamental security postures are unchanged.

A critical element in successful transmission of track two ideas is the existence of a policy "mentor"[42] (an official policymaker) who takes on such ideas and has the power to transfer concepts into actual policy. Of course, the stage has to be set before an official mentor can succeed in executing new policy, including preparing the public domain for the shift and working within a hospitable regional climate in which the

---

[42] On this concept of mentors to support track two dialogues, see Agha et al. (2003).

level of violence is relatively low. In other words, it must look advantageous for the official mentor to pursue cooperative policies at home and abroad; the ideas a mentor is willing to take on must be politically feasible and useful (a key precedent being the U.S.-Soviet dialogues and their influence on Gorbachev's thinking at a particularly crucial historical juncture). But examples of direct policy influence are more the exception than the rule. To better understand why this is the case, the following section will consider some of the challenges that track two dialogues face.

Limits of Track Two Dialogues

Obstacles to track two regional security dialogues can be found at three levels: the participating elites, the domestic contexts from which track two participants come, and the larger regional environment.

Two common problems emerge at the elite level: Either dialogues include the "wrong" type of people, or they include the "right" type of people with limited influence on official policy and little legitimacy in their domestic environments. The first problem relates to dialogues that are dominated by ideological individuals who do not believe in the value of cooperation with the adversary: They merely attend such forums to state well-known and deeply entrenched positions. Often, such individuals are government officials acting in an unofficial capacity who nonetheless feel the need to state conventional positions and are much more cautious about exploring new ideas and approaches to regional security for fear of censure at home.

Elites—official and unofficial—also may enter such processes with skeptical and even hostile positions because they come from security cultures that are adverse to cooperative security ideas. Mainstream positions in regions such as the Middle East and South Asia favor unilateralist and self-help notions that help foster zero-sum thinking. In such environments, it is difficult to find independent-minded elites who can break out of these conceptual frameworks and who are willing to consider new ideas, such as notions of mutual security that hold that a gain for one side can improve, rather than undermine, the position of the other. Analysts of track two dialogues in other regions, such as the Asia Pacific, have also observed that it is often difficult for track two to break new ground because the participating elites are too connected to governments and are thus unable to introduce new ideas in such dialogues, resulting in minimal impact on security policy (see Rüland, 2002, and Kraft, 2000).

On the other hand, the "right" type of participants—independent-minded individuals who will clearly express national perspectives and perceptions but still be open to listening to the other sides' views—can greatly improve the prospects for track two dialogues.[43] The problem is that such individuals—often coming from academia, think tanks, and NGOs—may have limited influence with official policymakers and are disconnected from grassroots groups or other broadly based societal movements. In short, such elites are often self-selected individuals who believe in the value of dialogue and conflict resolution but who do not necessarily represent the mainstream views of their societies. The converted are essentially talking to the converted.

Thus, the challenge of track two dialogues is to find a core group that includes the "right" type of individuals who also have influence and represent a broad spectrum of constituencies back home. But because track two is a long-term investment, organizers must consider including a wide range of participants—even those initially hostile to the process—because of the possibility that some of these participants may later assume important official positions in their countries.

However, even if organizers assemble an appropriate group, the participants may still reject a cooperative security agenda. Such elites may, through the process of dialogue and interaction in unofficial settings, develop views of the adversary that are *more* rather than less negative, or simply fail to buy into cooperative security concepts. If elites adopt such views, they have little incentive to spread the ideas any further and advocate new policies at home.

---

[43] International relations literature on persuasion suggests that arguing and persuasion are more likely to succeed among individuals who are less ideologically oriented. See, for instance, Checkel (2000), Crawford (2002), and Gibson (1998).

Resistance by participating elites may also arise out of resentment that outsiders are pushing the cooperative security agenda, even if the participants are supportive of the agenda itself. The perception of imposition from external actors to create a new regional security agenda can make regional elites uncomfortable with supporting the agenda and selling it at home to a wider audience. This suggests that form can be as critical as substance.

The challenge of selling new ideas and policies back home poses a second set of obstacles to track two dialogues. Cooperative security ideas are unlikely to be popular among populations that have experienced long-standing conflicts and high levels of violence. Cooperative postures are particularly dangerous for vulnerable regimes lacking legitimacy, as domestic opposition groups can use new security policies favoring cooperation with an adversary as political ammunition against a regime, particularly if such policy shifts are associated with Western agendas. We see great sensitivity to publicizing track two dialogues in regions such as the Middle East for this reason. While many track two dialogues would never get off the ground without operating discreetly, over time such sensitivity to public exposure can limit these processes' influence on security policy. At a certain point, the ideas emerging from the discussions need to "go public" and create a domestic discourse if a real shift in security policy is to come about.

Finally, the overall regional security environment can affect calculations about whether track two efforts can be introduced to a larger audience. Generally, in more favorable regional security environments—for example, when track one peace processes dealing with core bilateral conflicts such as Kashmir or Palestine appear to be moving forward—there is a greater chance for the development of an elite constituency favoring regional security cooperation and for exposure and acceptance at the broader societal level. Conversely, high levels of regional conflict and tension—such as periods following the breakdown of bilateral negotiations or during the absence of official dialogue among adversaries—make the transmission of cooperative security ideas to official policymakers and the wider public more difficult. This, of course, raises the dilemma that when unofficial channels may be most needed, they be most difficult to bring about.

While the complete resolution of core bilateral conflicts is not necessary for progress in regional security dialogues, the impression that such conflicts are advancing toward a resolution can greatly assist the potential of these dialogues to influence regional security thinking and, ultimately, policy. Setbacks in such processes or other destabilizing regional events (such as a regional conflict or a large-scale terrorist attack) can likewise impede the progress of track two security dialogues and limit their influence. Table 1.1 summarizes these general roles and limits. The next two chapters will apply these concepts to the Middle East and South Asia.

Table 1.1
Roles for Track Two Security Dialogues

	Socialization	Filtering	Policy Change
Facilitating Factors	Open-minded elites	Regional centers	Official policy mentors
	Limited media exposure during early stages	Participation by groups representing different segments of society and different views	Favorable regional security climate
	Conducive regional security environment (such as resumption of a peace process)	Indigenous track two activity	Reframing of track two idea as a national interest
		Favorable regional climate	Domestic support, including military, for new initiatives
Barriers	Ideological elites	Limited influence of elites with either government officials or broadly based social movements	Lack of official policy mentor
	Elites tied to government positions	Stigma of Western association and support	Limited elite influence—no transmission of track two ideas to official policy circle
	Dominant realist mind-set among security elites in competitive security environments	Domestic opposition to reconciliation with the adversary	Domestic opposition to new policy idea, particularly from military
	Adverse regional security developments (such as terrorist acts) disrupting ability of such processes to proceed	Adverse regional security environment	Adverse regional security environment

CHAPTER TWO

Regional Security Dialogues in the Middle East

Introduction

Security-related regional track two dialogues have become a permanent fixture in the Middle East since the early 1990s, although their nature and content have evolved over time.[1] The emergence of the first official regional security and arms control forum in 1992—the ACRS Working Group of the multilateral peace process—encouraged much regional thinking and cooperation on regional security and stimulated or accelerated a number of related track two efforts.

Despite some surprising progress, ACRS's Arab-Israeli focus inevitably led to serious divisions over contentious issues, particularly Israel's nuclear capabilities, halting the group's work by 1995.[2] ACRS's demise and the general deterioration of the Middle East peace process by the late 1990s—and the complete collapse of the Israeli-Palestinian peace process following the Al-Aksa intifada in September 2000—left unofficial forums as the only remaining venue for Arab-Israeli dialogue on regional security.

Although a number of track two dialogues managed to continue in the absence of an official peace process (and some even grew larger),

---

[1] Although some track two activities took place before the 1990s, the number of dialogues increased rapidly after the end of the Cold War and the 1991 Persian Gulf War. See Agha et al. (2003) for a discussion of track two activities in the 1980s. For the most comprehensive description of Middle East track two security programs up to 2001, see Yaffe (2001).

[2] For a detailed account of ACRS and the overall multilateral or regional peace process, see footnote 35 in Chapter One.

the absence of forward movement at the official level made track two efforts both more critical and more difficult. Although many participants valued the continued interaction in the absence of official contacts, the tense regional environment made it difficult to make progress on cooperative Arab-Israeli initiatives and increased the stakes for participants returning to domestic environments very much opposed to dialogue with the enemy at any level.

Track two groups increasingly found it challenging to meet in the region and to attract sufficient funding: Many groups, for example, began meeting in European capitals after 2000. Because Middle East track two efforts, particularly those with an Arab-Israeli dimension, never attracted broad regional support outside of the groups that participated in them, such efforts found little regional support. Some of the most prominent serial groups could not have survived without funding from the U.S. government or other, mostly Western, extraregional actors.

Because of these difficulties, Middle East track two forums over the past several years have been downplaying Arab-Israeli issues and instead focusing on Gulf regional security and Iran.[3] Some track two observers argue that an important aspect of such dialogues is to move regional actors beyond conceiving the problem of regional security as an extension of the Middle East peace process, since regional security is not limited to the Arab-Israeli arena (see, for example, Jones, 2005a).

Indeed, some regional track two forums are emerging from the Gulf, suggesting a new confidence among Gulf Cooperation Council states in asserting their interests in forums separate from the broader Arab agenda traditionally led by key Arab states such as Egypt.[4] As one observer of this trend notes, "The Egypt-inspired Arab League's insis-

---

[3] Another recent area for track two efforts, albeit bilateral rather than regional, is the upgrading of Israel's relations with NATO and the European Union. The German Marshall Fund has been organizing track two workshops specifically dedicated to this issue. For discussions about such ideas, see, for example, Asmus (2006), De Hoop Scheffer (2005), Fishman (2004), Prosser (2005), Lerman (2004), and Eran (2004).

[4] For a comprehensive argument favoring a subregional approach, see Yaffe (2004). For another argument in favor of a Gulf security system following an ARF model, see McMillan, Sokolsky, and Winner (2003).

tence on a regionwide focus reflects an eagerness on its part to remain engaged as a key actor, keep the foreign policies of the Arab Gulf states anchored in the Arab state system and prevent them from articulating a completely autonomous agenda. In reality, these pan-Arab norms have become irrelevant to the Gulf threat perceptions. . . . For them, the center of gravity of the Middle East has shifted from the Levant to the Gulf" (El-Hokayem and Legrenzi, 2006). Consequently, Gulf track two regional security forums generally avoid Arab-Israeli issues and concentrate instead on the challenges that their own subregion faces, a focus that has gained urgency in the aftermath of the Iraq war and its destabilizing consequences for many Gulf monarchies.

These more recent track two efforts underscore that regional security issues are not solely a function of the Arab-Israeli dispute, but they are also not without difficulty. It is not clear that Gulf-centered forums will make any faster progress nor that they can completely avoid the Arab-Israeli dispute. For example, the Saudi foreign minister has noted that Iran is not likely to give up its nuclear ambitions without a regional system in place that also addresses Israel and the U.S. presence in the area (Jones, 2005b).

Moreover, the position of Iran and Iraq in any future Gulf security forum is problematic. The current Iranian leadership has shown little interest in any form of regional cooperation, particularly with Arab Gulf neighbors desiring to rein in Iranian power and capabilities.[5] It is also questionable whether the small Gulf Cooperation Council (GCC) states would invite Iraq and Iran to join a regional grouping given that the institution was originally designed to balance both Iraq and Iran and was based on the common interests of Gulf monarchies. Growing concerns about rising Shi'a influence in Iraq and across the region will only reinforce such positions among Gulf Sunni states. Yet without the inclusion of Iran and Iraq, the viability of any Gulf forum would be questionable. So even Gulf-oriented track two forums will face signifi-

---

[5]   That said, some Iranian voices appear interested in multilateral regional security cooperation. See, for example, the 10-point proposal for a Persian Gulf security cooperation council by the former secretary of the Supreme Council for National Security, Hassan Ruhani, discussed in Afrasiabi (2007). Also see Zarif (2007).

cant challenges in their efforts to create a cooperative regional security framework.

Many hoped that a resumption of an Israeli-Palestinian peace process following the unilateral Israeli withdrawal from Gaza in the summer of 2005 would strengthen and revive broader regional track two dialogues. But the Hamas victory in the January 2006 Palestinian elections again dimmed hopes for a renewed peace process, at least on the Palestinian track. The transition from Ariel Sharon to Ehud Olmert as prime minister of Israel in March 2006, the Israeli war with Hezbollah in the summer of 2006, and the Hamas takeover of power in Gaza in June 2007 have created additional uncertainties about the future of the peace process.

A renewed peace process would certainly boost track two efforts and make it more likely that cooperative security concepts and activities would reach broader audiences and perhaps even influence policy over time. Yet the constant potential for violence between Arabs and Israelis—and the escalation of violence throughout the region in the aftermath of the Iraq war—underscores the need for continued track two dialogues on key regional security issues. Because of their long-term nature, track two forums can serve as incubators for ideas that may eventually see the light of day during more politically opportune periods. However, the record of such dialogues to date in the Middle East suggests serious limitations in their ability to influence broader public discourse in the region even during more hopeful times in Arab-Israeli relations.

Overview of Dialogues

Although nongovernmental actors—universities, research centers, think tanks, and NGOs—usually organize track two workshops, the United States and other Western governments have funded many regional projects, and most are conducted in English. In the 1990s the U.S. Department of State and the U.S. Department of Energy were the primary funders for Middle East track two, but more recently the U.S. Department of Defense (DoD) has taken over as the central funder. For example, one of the largest regional track two dialogues receives approximately $1.2 million annually for its activities through the annual DoD authorization bill.[6]

Because track two workshops are expensive (a one-week workshop in the region can cost up to $300,000), governmental financial support is critical to the continuation of many efforts (Yaffe, 2001, p. 23). Other extraregional governments and some private foundations also provide funding for track two activities, particularly those including Iranians, because U.S. government funds cannot support Iranian attendance.[7] Some estimate total track two spending on Middle East projects—governmental and nongovernmental—at approximately $2.5 million annually.[8]

The number of track two participants has risen dramatically over the years. A U.S. State Department official who helped organize many Middle East track two dialogues (and maintained lists of track two participants) estimates that 750 regional and extraregional elites participated in track two activities during the 1990s, of whom 200 were from the military, including 40 who were general officer grade (Yaffe, 2001, p. 15). Today, estimates for individuals who have participated in one or more track two activities related to the Middle East are in the thousands.[9] During the 1990s, approximately 100 track two events were organized, averaging one activity per month (Yaffe, 2001, p. 15). Although the pace has slowed for broader regional forums, recent track two activism in the Gulf suggests that frequent and regular track two activity continues to define the regional landscape.

---

[6] Phone interview with Michael Yaffe, March 20, 2006.

[7] Extraregional states such as Australia, Canada, Finland, Germany, the Netherlands, Norway, Sweden, Switzerland, and the United Kingdom collectively contribute approximately $500,000 annually to track two efforts. Private foundations also make regular contributions, but mostly to single workshops rather than to serial programs. The most active foundations funding track two activities include the Ford Foundation, the W. Alton Jones Foundation, the Rockefeller Foundation, and the John D. and Catherine T. MacArthur Foundation (Yaffe, 2001, p. 23).

[8] Based on interviews with various track two organizers, March 2006.

[9] Interviews with track two organizers in March 2006.

Because of the large number of regional track two activities, the following review highlights the most prominent and ongoing regional dialogues, determined by the frequency with which they were mentioned during interviews with Middle East track two participants and organizers.[10]

UCLA and the Institute on Global Conflict and Cooperation

Among the most prominent track two processes in the Middle East are those organized by the University of California, Los Angeles (UCLA), political science professor Steven Spiegel and related activity organized by the University of California's Institute on Global Conflict and Cooperation (IGCC). These activities include a broad-based dialogue group currently meeting three times per year in Europe—involving up to 250 participants per meeting—as well as a smaller military-to-military dialogue meeting semi-annually, including, at times, in Middle East capitals when security and political considerations allow. The military dialogues include active-duty and retired generals from nearly every Arab country, Turkey, and Israel. (Iranian representatives participate in the broad-based meetings but not in the military dialogues.)

IGCC initially sponsored track two workshops in the 1990s related to the work of the multilateral peace process working groups (addressing issues such as regional security and arms control, economic development, water, the environment, and refugees). But with the demise of that process in the late 1990s, since 1997 IGCC's track two activities have focused on the military-to-military dialogues. The project brings senior regional military officers together to exchange views and ideas about regional security and to expand the group of officials who are familiar with regional arms control issues. In fact, more mili-

---

[10] Complete data for each group—funding sources, participants, and number and location of meetings—is not accessible in all cases due to the sensitivity of this subject. For example, at times I purposely omit information on meeting locations to protect the safety of individuals who may participate in a particular group. Because of political sensitivities and fear for the safety and well-being of participants, track two organizers are often reluctant to divulge information about the workings of their groups and often instruct participants to protect the information as well. This makes obtaining detailed data on track two activities extremely difficult and explains the uneven nature of data collection across various groups.

tary officers have been involved with this project than with the official ACRS Working Group. The topics covered include military balances in the region, weapon effects, military doctrines, arms control, counter-proliferation measures, military ethics, and military education. Some meetings involve paper presentations, with participants sharing their country's regional security perspectives and threat perceptions. Other meetings have focused on operational issues, such as a code of conduct for military behavior in the Middle East.

Professor Spiegel's broader track two series has been meeting since 1995 and has grown significantly over the years. The group has become so large that it rarely meets in a full plenary session format and instead breaks up into a number of separate working groups that focus on different dimensions of regional security, including economic development, democracy, Mediterranean security, Gulf security, general security challenges (including weapons of mass destruction [WMD]), Israeli-Palestinian relations, women's issues, and technology.[11]

In addition to the ongoing working groups, the UCLA process created a number of specialized task forces to consider specific issues in a small, "invitation-only" format that is intended to produce a concrete product within a specified time. For example, in 2003 a task force was formed to develop a draft regional security charter for the Middle East. Peter Jones (a Canadian official who also participates in track two meetings in his academic capacity) led the effort. The bulk of the funding for the larger UCLA process comes from the U.S. and Greek governments, although the funding for some of the task forces is independent. Many of the track two working groups continue their interactions throughout the year between the larger meetings, and some

---

[11] In the late 1990s UCLA also sponsored a track two project with the National Center for Middle East Studies in Cairo. This track two group began meeting three to four times per year in Cairo starting in 1999, with the ultimate goal being the creation of an Association of National Security Centers. The political setbacks on the Israeli-Palestinian track prevented such an association from materializing, but the Near East South Asia Center for Strategic Studies (NESA) at the National Defense University in Washington, D.C., has since created a network of regional security centers to encourage regional research collaboration. According to NESA professor Michael Yaffe, 30 regional centers have signed up for the network (phone interview with Michael Yaffe, March 20, 2006).

are now working to produce publications to disseminate their ideas to broader audiences.

Taken together, the UCLA and IGCC activities have maintained and expanded relationships among regional security elites even in the absence of an official arms control process and despite a difficult regional environment. However, because of the sensitivity about such meetings and security concerns, the groups have generally not been able to meet in the region. That said, Spiegel began organizing a more public track two dialogue in 2006 focused on economic development issues, with the first meeting taking place in Doha, Qatar, in late January 2006 (the conference was cosponsored by the Qatari foreign ministry and UCLA's Ronald W. Burkle Center for International Relations).[12] The Doha conference included business, governmental, and academic leaders from 14 Arab states, Israel, the United States, Europe, and Asia and focused on issues such as energy development, regional banking, trade, and regional reform in areas including education, women's empowerment, and enhancing freedoms (Speigel, 2006).

The Stockholm International Peace Research Institute (SIPRI)

SIPRI sponsored a number of track two projects in the 1990s, including attempts to develop CBMs for the Gulf region, an electronic network on security issues and arms control, and the development of a regional security regime. The regional security regime project led to a high-profile report, prepared by the project organizer (Jones 1998). A group of established regional and extraregional security experts (including Iranian and former ACRS participants) met for four sessions over an 18-month period spanning 1997 and 1998 to prepare the report. Drawing on lessons from security regimes in other regions, the report developed guiding principles for the establishment of a security regime in the Middle East. The report, published in December 1998, was widely distributed throughout the region, and the project leader, Peter Jones, toured the Middle East to share the report's findings with regional parties.

---

[12] For conference details, see UCLA Ronald W. Burkle Center for International Relations (2006).

Although SIPRI had ended some of these projects by 1999, much of its work continued through other forums. The University of Toronto's Munk Center for International Relations, with funding from the Canadian government, ran the electronic network project; currently the IGCC holds the reins, with funding from the UCLA track two project budget. The network allows for private and secure communication on issues related to regional security among a broad group of participants (from most Arab states, Iran, Turkey, and Israel).

More recently, the Canadian and Danish governments—in response to regional interest—sponsored a track two effort to establish a regional charter, drawing on principles developed in the previous SIPRI report. The project developed a consortium of research institutes from the region and hosted a series of conferences that considered the creation of a framework for regional cooperation and security in the Middle East and North Africa.[13] This consortium has met several times and plans to produce a public report of its work, essentially a second volume to the first SIPRI report.[14]

The Search for Common Ground

In 1991, the Search for Common Ground launched the Initiative for Peace and Cooperation in the Middle East, since called the Search for Common Ground in the Middle East.[15] The Washington- and Brussels-based NGO (with a regional office in Amman, Jordan) is among the most experienced organizations promoting peace-building and conflict-resolution dialogues in the Middle East. The Middle East project established a number of working groups over the years, includ-

---

[13] See Al-Ahram Center for Political and Strategic Studies (2004) and Pugwash Online (undated [b]). The research institutes include the Al-Ahram Center (Cairo), the Gulf Research Center (Dubai), the Institut Diplomatique et des Relations Internationales (Algiers), and the Centre Tarik Ibn Zyad (Rabat). The Regional Centre on Conflict Prevention at the Jordanian Institute of Diplomacy has also joined the consortium, and the sponsors expect others to join soon as well (correspondence with consortium participant, April 2006).

[14] Based on correspondence with a participant, April 2006.

[15] For a detailed study of the Search for Common Ground's activities in the Middle East, see Funk (2000). For an updated list of program activities in the Middle East until 2006, see Search for Common Ground (2006).

ing one focused specifically on regional security (other working groups focus on issues such as civil society, conflict resolution, economics, and the media). Its current agenda concentrates primarily on Middle East media projects and regional dialogue and cooperation initiatives.

Over the years, the Search for Common Ground's security group has focused on a variety of issues, including WMD, the Gulf, and Arab-Israeli security. The group has addressed specific issues such as confidence-building in Lebanon, the redeployment of Israeli troops to the West Bank and Gaza, Israeli-Jordanian relations, Iraq-Kuwait reconciliation, and an outline for a Syrian-Israeli peace agreement. From 1992 to 1994 a group of Israelis and Syrians affiliated with its security group engaged in a series of meetings and almost came to an agreement on security arrangements that, if successful, might have helped bridge the gap in the official Israeli-Syrian peace process.[16] The security group's activities also produced several publications, many authored by project participants (Eisendorf, 1995; Schiff, Khalidi, and Agha, 1994; Levran and Shiyyab, 1994; and Agha and Levran, 1992). Since 1992, the Middle East project has also produced a quarterly newsletter, the *Bulletin of Regional Cooperation in the Middle East*,[17] to disseminate information about governmental and nongovernmental cooperative activities in the region.

Currently active projects in the Middle East regional dialogue and cooperation arena include the Middle East Consortium on Infectious Disease Surveillance (MECIDS) group, which since 2003 has facilitated regional cooperation against biological attacks and natural disease outbreaks. MECIDS has facilitated the sharing of data and cooperation among Israelis, Jordanians, and Palestinians about disease outbreaks and the threat of avian influenza, or bird flu (Search for Common Ground, 2003). Another cooperative regional security project, the Middle East Chemical Risks Consortium (CRC), began

---

[16] Interview with Jordanian security analyst, Amman, January 21, 2001, and interview with American participant, Washington, D.C., January 11, 2001.

[17] Since January 2004, the *Bulletin* has been published electronically at the Search for Common Ground Web site. As of July 18, 2007: http://www.sfcg.org/

in 2003 and published a book prepared by the project's participating regional researchers (Egyptian, Israeli, Jordanian, and Palestinian).[18] The book consists of case studies that detail a local incident and the lessons that emerged for chemical emergency response. The CRC project grew out of earlier WMD work in the security group, and its goals include improving the capacity of regional actors to manage chemical incidents while building confidence among regional participants. With its focus on chemical incidents, the CRC is a companion project to Search's MECIDS group and reflects Search's overall mission to move adversaries away from conflictual approaches and toward cooperative solutions addressing areas of common concern.

DePaul University

Beginning in 1995, DePaul University sponsored, with funding primarily from the U.S. government (specifically, the Department of Energy), a trilateral project among Egyptians, Israelis, and Jordanians called the "Mid-East Group of Experts on the Establishment of a Regional Security Regime in the Middle East Including the Elimination of Weapons of Mass Destruction (WMD)." The idea for the project emanated from high-level Egyptian elites, who wanted to create a dialogue with the Israelis that focused explicitly on the issue of Israel's nuclear capability (the idea was taken up by an Egyptian-born law professor at DePaul). The project sponsored one to two meetings per year, which usually took place in Egypt, Israel, or Jordan. Most of its participants were affiliated with a strategic institute in their respective countries (e.g., the National Center for Middle East Studies in Cairo, the Jaffee Center for Strategic Studies in Tel Aviv, the Hassan Council in Amman).

All of the national centers that participated in the project have links to officials in their respective countries. In the early meetings, the participants worked on a manual of WMD in the Middle East, but the parties were unable to agree on a proposed document that would establish a framework for the elimination of WMD from the region.

---

[18] Meyers (2003). The regional authors are Hassan Dweik, Derar Melkawi, Major General (ret.) Salah Eldin Selim Mohamed, Jean Negreanu, Shlomo Rosenberg, Yair Sharan, and Major General (ret.) Mohammad K. Shiyyab.

Progress was made, however, on the definition of the region, guiding principles for a regional security regime, and frameworks for future regional security institutions. The parties discussed ideas for regional institutions, such as a Middle East security council that would include regional defense ministers and a Middle East disarmament and arms control organization. The group also studied other regional models, such as ASEAN, to draw lessons for the Middle East. But political tensions and growing concerns from the Israeli government that the group was being used by the Egyptians to pressure Israel impeded the group's further progress.[19] It ceased meeting in 2000.

United Nations Institute for Disarmament Research (UNIDIR)

UNIDIR began supporting track two activities in the Middle East in 1993, producing a number of publications, including (with U.S. Department of State funding) two handbooks explaining the major terms, concepts, and agreements related to arms control and verification (United Nations Institute for Disarmament Research, 2002a, 2002b). In September 1998 UNIDIR co-hosted (again, with U.S. Department of State funding) a workshop with Sandia National Laboratories' Cooperative Monitoring Center (CMC) on the role of commercial satellites and aerial imagery in arms control, economic development, environmental enhancement, and natural-resource exploration in the Middle East region. Arab and Israeli regional experts discussed the possibilities and limits of such technology in their region, particularly in relation to verification of regional arms control agreements, and produced a publication from the effort (United Nations Institute for Disarmament Research, 1999). UNIDIR's track two efforts have also produced several other publications related to regional arms control and security (see, for example, Prawitz and Leonard, 1996, and Leonard et al., 1995).

---

[19] For details on the Israeli government's reservations about this group's activities, see Agha et al. (2003, p. 131).

Cooperative Monitoring Center

In addition to its collaboration with UNIDIR, the CMC at Sandia National Laboratories runs a number of projects and hosts a visiting fellows program that provides technical support and education for regional experts on regional arms control and verification issues. At one of its earliest Middle East workshops, held at Sandia in July 1994 (cosponsored with IGCC and largely funded by the U.S. Department of Energy), the CMC focused on the use of technical monitoring tools and the sharing of collected information to facilitate regional agreements. The workshop brought academic, military, and governmental experts together from Israel, Egypt, Qatar, Oman, and Kuwait. As a report from the workshop explains, the goal of such CMC efforts is to "provide a neutral forum where international and regional representatives can meet to share extensive U.S. experience in monitoring and verification and explore ways that technology can facilitate regional confidence building" (Pregenzer et al., 1995). Activities in these types of workshops include technical demonstrations of verification exercises and monitoring systems through the center's technology laboratories.

In another CMC workshop, Jordanians and Israelis examined how to monitor borders and subsequently published papers on border monitoring and technology (see, for example, Qojas, 1999). As part of the project, the scholars traveled to Washington, D.C., to share their work and ideas with policymakers. In 1996, the center hosted Jordan, Egypt, and Israel to examine options for a WMD free zone (WMDFZ) in the Middle East and the role of technology in monitoring such an agreement. As mentioned, the program also joined with UNIDIR in 1998 to examine satellite imagery and its role in monitoring peace agreements, including water and environmental issues. In 1996 and 1997, the CMC collaborated with the U.S. Department of State and provided regional participants a two-week course on regional arms control.[20] More than 50 regional officials participated in this training course.

---

[20] The U.S. Air War College has also sponsored workshops to educate military elites about ACRS-related activities. In 1998, for example, the Air War College sponsored a conference on Middle East security and WMD proliferation. The purpose of such seminars is to educate future military leaders about regional security issues and arms control techniques, with the

In more recent years the CMC has also initiated projects focused on confidence-building in the Gulf and the engagement of Iraqi scientists as Iraq struggles to rebuild its infrastructure.[21] At the suggestion of regional experts, CMC also helped establish a regional cooperative monitoring center at the Royal Scientific Society in Amman, Jordan, which officially opened in October 2003. The CMC in Amman is largely modeled on the CMC at Sandia and runs a number of training programs and workshops to promote the role of science and technology to address nonproliferation, arms control, and other security challenges.[22]

In the spring of 2004, for example, the CMC in Amman hosted a workshop on border security operators that included 35 military and civilian officials from a variety of regional states. In 2005, it hosted a training workshop for Iraqi scientists on seismological analysis, as well as a regional workshop on border security and counterterrorism that included participants from Iraq, Jordan, Kuwait, Saudi Arabia, and Turkey. In 2006, workshop topics included regional biosecurity and biosafety (attended by representatives from 13 Arab countries) and cooperative monitoring training (with participants from Jordan, Israel, and Egypt).

In collaboration with the Verification Research, Training and Information Center (an independent NGO), the CMC in Amman held a meeting in August 2006 (with funding from the British government) on approaches to national implementation of nuclear, chemical, and biological weapon agreements that included representatives from a number of Arab states and Iran. At the CMCs in both Sandia and Amman, the expansion of confidence-building activities beyond the

---

hope that they will make these issues a priority when they are promoted to high-ranking positions within their respective governments.

[21] For a complete listing of CMC projects in the Middle East, see Sandia National Laboratories' CMC Web site (as of July 18, 2007):
http://www.cmc.sandia.gov/

[22] For an overview of CMC-Amman work, see its Web site (as of July 18, 2007):
http://www.cmc-amman.gov.jo/main.htm

Arab-Israeli context to the Gulf, including Iraq and Iran, mirrors a similar shift in focus found in other track two efforts.

Canadian-Sponsored Maritime Activities

After the demise of the ACRS Working Group, the Canadian government (with support from the U.S. Department of State) sponsored track two workshops in the maritime area (Canada previously mentored maritime CBMs in ACRS), with activities coordinated by a former Canadian naval officer. The objective of the workshops was to avoid losing the progress made in ACRS, particularly its work on regional search-and-rescue (SAR) and incident-at-sea (INCSEA) activities. Other issues addressed in maritime track two workshops included marine environmental protection and response, international ship and port security, and piracy and armed robbery against ships. Cooperative projects in the maritime area became a popular component of track two activities because the international maritime culture provided a powerful tool for dialogue and cooperation on humanitarian issues.[23]

The Canadian Coast Guard started the Maritime Safety Colloquium (MarSaf) for Middle East naval officers in 1997. MarSaf convened again in 1998 at the Canadian Coast Guard College in Sydney, Canada, with the participation of regional maritime officers and specialists from nine Middle East nations. The MarSaf meetings moved to the region in 1999, with Jordan agreeing to host the meeting in Aqaba under the sponsorship of the Royal Jordanian Naval Force. The MarSaf meeting scheduled for Tangier, Morocco, in November 2000 was never held because of violence following the outbreak of the second intifada in September 2000. The group did manage to meet again, however, in Aqaba in 2001 and then in Qatar in 2002. After missing a meeting in 2003, MarSaf held its last meeting in October 2004, again in Aqaba.

In the early sessions, the program promoted concrete exercises in SAR coordination in the region, including simulation exercises in which Arabs and Israelis were able to coordinate activity in realistic, crisis-like settings. In recent years, however, the discussion has been no different than at conventional international maritime safety meetings.

---

[23] On the advantages of maritime cooperation, see Griffiths (2000) and Jones (1996).

The project also published the *Maritime Safety Newsletter* and proceedings from its meetings.[24]

MarSaf encouraged not only cooperation on technical issues in a collegial working environment, but also informal dialogue among participants through cultural activities and excursions, creating a vast network of maritime specialists from the region (Mann, 2002). Alumni of the program now number in the hundreds (Mann, 2002). Although the U.S. government supported the project, the Canadians took the lead in this area and supplied the bulk of the expertise and funding. However, as of late 2006, the networking process appeared to have lost momentum for bureaucratic rather than political reasons. Consequently, despite almost a decade of considerable progress, the future of the project is unclear.

The U.S. Geological Survey and Lawrence Livermore National Laboratory: Regional Seismic Monitoring Cooperation Project

Beginning in 1992, this project has held nearly two workshops per year, organized primarily by the U.S. Geological Survey and, since 1995, Lawrence Livermore National Laboratory (funded largely by the U.S. Department of State and Department of Energy but under the auspices of the United Nations Educational, Scientific and Cultural Organisation [UNESCO]). Its aim is to promote scientific cooperation on seismology concerns that can enhance regional security. One of its earlier projects, for example, was the creation a database of Middle East seismic events that could provide a baseline for distinguishing between natural and human-caused seismic events, such as nuclear tests. The project has also sought to facilitate economic and urban planning in the region to reduce the losses associated with earthquakes and to educate regional parties about the technologies needed for monitoring the

---

[24] For details regarding these maritime security activities, see the Centre for Foreign Policy Studies of Dalhousie University's Web site (as of June 14, 2007):
http://centreforforeignpolicystudies.dal.ca/index.php
Publications related to this work are listed under David Griffiths in the section "no longer available" (but copies can be ordered from the center directly) on the following Web link (as of June 25, 2007):
http://centreforforeignpolicystudies.dal.ca/pubs.php#marsec

Comprehensive Test Ban Treaty (CTBT). Other technical workshop topics have included disaster preparation, earthquake damage assessment, and building codes.

Most of the workshops and training sessions take place in the region. Project participants from throughout the region have shared national data on seismic activities with a clearinghouse in Europe and produced a joint study on the November 1995 Gulf of Aqaba earthquake. For this study, even Israel and Saudi Arabia exchanged seismic data. These efforts have also produced joint exercises, such as planned explosions in the Aqaba region. The idea of such exercises is to help regionals understand differences between nuclear testing and natural seismic activity and to increase transparency and avoid misperceptions that could escalate toward conflict.

As is common in other track two venues, more recent seismology work has specifically targeted the Gulf region. Livermore has worked with institutions in the Gulf to organize a series of technical meetings called the Gulf Seismic Forum, focusing on earthquake-hazard mitigation in the region.[25] These meetings began in 2004 in the United Arab Emirates and have continued in other Gulf capitals, including Muscat, Oman, and Kuwait City, Kuwait. These meetings are funded mainly by their regional hosts and do not involve either UNESCO or the U.S. Geological Survey.[26]

European-Sponsored Activities

In addition to contributing funding for many of the previously mentioned track two activities, various European governments and institutions also sponsor their own track two workshops. Wilton Park, an executive agency with links to the British government, organizes four annual conferences on the Middle East. The Danish government has been particularly active in recent years in supporting various track two efforts, particularly those focused on establishing a regional security charter. The Canada-based Pugwash Conferences on Science and

---

[25] Email correspondence with Keith Nakanishi, seismologist at Lawrence Livermore National Laboratory, December 14, 2006.

[26] Email correspondence with Nakanishi, 2006.

World Affairs sponsors numerous workshops dedicated to Middle East and Gulf security issues, often in conjunction with European sponsors such as the Swedish government and in association with regional and international policy institutes.[27] The Organization for Security and Co-Operation in Europe (OSCE) hosts a Mediterranean seminar once a year to foster regional dialogue on security issues. Germany also supports an annual conference focused on Middle East security topics, the Kronberg Conference.

The establishment of the official Barcelona Process in 1995— sponsored by the European Union and intended to promote European-Mediterranean cooperation on political, economic, and cultural affairs—also led to a number of workshops that mirror its official work (Vasconcelos and Joffe, 2000). For example, the Euro-Mediterranean Study Commission (EuroMeSCo) project, begun in 1996, brings together foreign policy research centers from around the Mediterranean region to, as the Barcelona Declaration states, "establish a network for more intensive [regional] cooperation." The Middle East members of the network include strategic and international studies institutes in Algeria, Egypt, Israel, Jordan, Lebanon, Palestine, Morocco, Tunisia, Syria, and Turkey. EuroMeSCo has a secretariat in Lisbon and a Web site,[28] providing a forum for dialogue and discussion on regional security issues.

Gulf Security Track Two Forums

Although one prominent track two group—Gulf/2000—has been operating since 1993, the demise of the Israeli-Palestinian peace process and difficulties in generating regionwide discussions on regional security have contributed to the growth of other unofficial Gulf forums in recent years.[29] While the groups discussed here all address the Iranian nuclear issue and the general role of Iran in regional security

---

[27]   On Pugwash's Middle East activities, see Pugwash Online (undated [c]).

[28]   For more information, see the EuroMesCo Web site. As of June 14, 2007: http://www.euromesco.net/

[29]   A number of analysts have also been focusing on Gulf regional security options, including a NATO-like regional defense alliance. See, for example, Indyk (2004) and McMillan, Sokolsky, and Winner (2003, pp. 161–175).

affairs, Iran-specific track two dialogues have also emerged since the 2003 Iraq war and the standoff with Iran over its nuclear ambitions.[30] The International Institute for Strategic Studies (IISS), in conjunction with the government of Bahrain, has also initiated a Gulf dialogue project that brings together security officials from the Gulf (many represented at the foreign minister level) to discuss regional security issues and challenges.[31] This forum seeks to model itself on ARF, suggesting that the Asian example for security dialogue may be more relevant to Gulf affairs than European models (International Institute for Strategic Studies, 2006). Although the IISS Gulf dialogue more closely resembles an official rather than a track two process, its development further underscores the willingness of Gulf states to shift their focus away from regionwide forums toward Gulf-specific venues.

The following overview of Gulf-related track two projects addresses three particularly prominent Gulf forums that are relatively transparent and well documented, but this overview is by no means exhaustive of the efforts emerging in this area.

Gulf/2000. Created in 1993 to foster regional dialogue on Gulf-related security issues, Gulf/2000 is based at Columbia University under the direction of Gary Sick, a former White House advisor in the Ford, Carter, and Reagan administrations and an expert on U.S.-Iran relations. The project received initial funding from the W. Alton Jones Foundation and is currently supported by a number of other private foundations, including the Ford Foundation, the John D. and Catherine T. MacArthur Foundation, the Carnegie Corporation of New York, the Open Society Institute of the Soros Foundation, and the ExxonMobil Foundation.[32] The project does not receive any governmental funds, maximizing its flexibility to encourage regionwide dialogue.

---

[30] These efforts are too new to document in any detail here. But conversations and email correspondence with participants and organizers confirm that Iran-specific track two dialogues are taking place on a regular basis. Geoffrey Kemp of the Nixon Center is leading one major effort, and the United Nations Peace Academy is sponsoring another series of meetings.

[31] The first summit was held in Bahrain in 2004. For further details, see International Institute for Strategic Studies (2006).

[32] For a detailed overview of Gulf/2000, see its Web site. As of July 18, 2007: http://gulf2000.columbia.edu

The flagship project of this group is its electronic network, which connects over 1,000 scholars and analysts who have a professional interest in the Gulf region, allowing ideas and debates to circulate online, often among influential elites with considerable access to their own government's decisionmaking circles. This is one of the few places where Israelis and Iranians, for example, can openly exchange views on critical security perceptions and beliefs. The electronic network also offers an online library with valuable research resources and links for the community of experts. In addition to its electronic network, Gulf/2000 has also sponsored at least 10 international conferences and workshops on current and historical Gulf security issues. Many of the papers from these conferences and workshops appear in volumes edited by Gary Sick and Gulf/2000 deputy director Lawrence Potter (see Sick and Potter, 1997, 2002, and 2004; a fourth volume, *The Persian Gulf in History*, is scheduled for publication in 2007).

Stanley Foundation/Institute for Near East and Gulf Military Analysis (INEGMA). In January 2004 the Stanley Foundation, in association with INEGMA, sponsored a track two workshop in Dubai focused on examining alternative regional security frameworks for the Gulf.[33] The Stanley Foundation, a private, nonpartisan foundation focusing primarily on peace and security issues, promotes what it terms "principled multilateralism" (or working with others across differences to create fair and lasting solutions) in its track two dialogues. INEGMA is also an NGO that offers media, research, and consultation services in security and defense issues and was founded by Riad Kahwaji, a Middle East defense analyst specializing in Gulf security.[34] Workshop participants came from Gulf Arab monarchies, Iran, Iraq, other Middle East states, Europe, and the United States.

---

[33] The conference report and resulting papers are all published in Kraig (2004). For more information about the two sponsoring organizations, see their Web sites. As of June 14, 2007:
http://www.stanleyfoundation.org
http://www.inegma.com

[34] For example, for Kahwaji's views on the Iranian nuclear issue and Gulf security, see Kahwaji (2006).

The Stanley/INEGMA Gulf security group met for a second workshop in September 2005 in Dubai (following a smaller meeting with only GCC and American participants in May 2005).[35] The larger meeting also included participants from South Asia (India and Pakistan) as well as from Japan and China to explore Asian interests in the Gulf and their implications for regional security. The group's meeting in Muscat, Oman, in June 2006 addressed pressing Gulf security challenges, such as the conflict in Iraq and the Iranian nuclear issue. According to the group's organizer, Michael Kraig, the Oman meeting was well attended by Iranians from a variety of factions.[36]

The group's central objective is to outline alternative regional security options, including the consideration of cooperative multilateral regional security frameworks, to improve security and stability in the Gulf region. The project organizes workshops and commissions papers to explore such ideas and encourage regional exchange. More recently, the initiative has focused on encouraging a U.S.-Iranian détente and a more cooperative Gulf security structure, as well as on addressing the misperceptions and other impediments to the creation of a cooperative security system in the region. The Stanley Foundation also envisions future Middle East projects that will involve Turkey more directly in the dialogue as well as supplemental bilateral and trilateral discussions (among Arab Gulf states, Iran, and the United States) to further the cooperative security agenda and build confidence among regional adversaries.

The Gulf Research Center (GRC). Another Gulf initiative emerged in 2004 from the GRC, a privately funded nongovernmental think tank based in Dubai.[37] This initiative focuses on the creation of a Gulf Weapons of Mass Destruction Free Zone (GWMDFZ) as the first stage toward a more comprehensive Middle East WMD free

---

[35] A summary report of the conference discussions is published in Stanley Foundation (2005).

[36] Phone interview with Michael Kraig of the Stanley Foundation, November 28, 2006.

[37] For updates on this track two effort, see Gulf Research Center (2006), as well as the rest of the center's Web site. As of June 15, 2007:
http://www.grc.ae

zone.[38] High-level participants from the region (acting in an unofficial capacity) as well as regional experts launched the initiative at their first meeting in Dubai in December 2004, where they discussed WMD proliferation and its effects in the Gulf. The initiative includes participants from the six states of the GCC in addition to Iran, Iraq, and Yemen, the nations that together compose the suggested scope of the proposed WMD free zone. The group met a second time in Stockholm in May 2005, a meeting cosponsored and jointly financed by SIPRI (which was funded in part by the European Union).[39]

GRC's third meeting took place in Dubai in May 2006, cohosted with the Verification Research, Training and Information Centre (VERTIC), with funding from the UK Foreign and Commonwealth Office. VERTIC's role in the meeting was to help regional actors understand the measures they would need to take at the national level to comply with disarmament or arms control treaties as well as the overall importance of implementation to the arms control process.

The GRC initiative has received high-level notice, with the secretary-general of the GCC endorsing the idea at the GCC summit in Abu Dhabi in December 2005 (Al Attiya, 2005). The Kuwaiti government also expressed support for the initiative at the December 2005 summit ("The State of Kuwait," 2005). Given this support, the GRC believes that the initiative may be ripe for movement from track two to track one negotiations.[40] That said, a harshly worded letter from Secretary-General Amr Moussa of the Arab League to the secretary-general of the GCC regarding this initiative suggests that the idea will face formidable regional opposition. In his letter, Moussa characterized the initiative as being "falsehood masquerading as right" and suggested that its backers are influenced by international forces (including "non-Arab states with policies known for their bias to nuclearized Israel and

---

[38] For detailed information about this initiative, see Gulf Research Center (2005). For a broader discussion regarding a GWMDFZ within the context of a Middle East security architecture, see Jones (2005b).

[39] The information regarding these meetings is based on email correspondence with a researcher at the GRC on March 14, 2006, and March 27, 2006.

[40] Email correspondence with a researcher at the GRC, March 14, 2006.

its protection") and are undermining collective Arab efforts by drawing attention away from Israel's nuclear position (Moussa, 2005). This letter, along with a strongly worded response from the state of Kuwait ("Memorandum," 2005), further underscores the tensions between regionwide Arab norms and an increasing inclination of Gulf states to follow their own subregional interests.[41]

Table 2.1 summarizes all of the Middle East track two processes discussed above.

Roles

Socialization

In track two dialogues, outside parties typically promote a standard set of ideas and norms—usually cooperative security concepts in the Middle East case—in efforts to socialize regional actors toward thinking about regional security in new ways. The first step in this process is to emphasize that the dialogue itself is important as a means to better understand the other participants' positions (e.g., threat perceptions, policies, red-lines). Such understanding may make actors more willing to engage in regional security cooperation if threat perceptions of regional neighbors are reduced.[42] Another aspect of socialization is the educational value of such dialogues, which discuss in depth substantive concepts such as CBMs, deterrence theory, and cooperative security.

---

[41] Al Attiya (2005), "The State of Kuwait" (2005), Moussa (2005), and "Memorandum" (2005) are all included in "The Gulf as a WMD Free Zone: Dossier of Official Documents and Statements," an undated GRC document on file with the author.

[42] Humanizing the enemy is another often-cited role for track two dialogues, which certainly did take place in Arab-Israeli context. This "humanizing" aspect, however, can be and often is overstated. While some individuals have developed sincere friendships, mistrust and tension continue to prevail in Arab-Israeli dialogues, and the participants tend to congregate as national delegations whenever possible. Moreover, many of the Gulf participants (with the exception of the Iranians) are cautious and quiet in meetings and generally do not interact unnecessarily with the Israeli participants. For an elaboration of the humanization concept, drawn from social psychology, see Funk (2000). Among the more important features of humanizing the enemy is viewing the "other" in more personal rather than abstract terms and breaking down the in-group versus out-group dichotomy.

Table 2.1
Track Two Regional Security Dialogues in the Middle East

Track Two Group	Primary Sponsor(s)	Period of Activity	Key Regional Participants' Countries of Origin	Discussion Topics
UCLA and the Institute on Global Conflict and Cooperation	U.S. government, Greek government, private foundations	Early 1990–present	Arab League states, Israel, Iran, and Turkey	Regional security, proliferation, mil-mil dialogues, economic development, civil society, Israeli-Palestinian conflict
Search for Common Ground	U.S. government, European governments, the EU, and private foundations (including Nuclear Threat Initiative, Compton Foundation, Sagner Family Fund, Foundation for Middle East Peace)	1991–present	Arab League states, Israel, Iran, and Turkey	Security, civil society, conflict resolution, economics, media
Stockholm International Peace Research Institute	Private foundations, European governments	1990s (continuing in other forums today)	Arab League states, Israel, Iran, and Turkey	Regional security charter, CBMs in Gulf, electronic arms control network
DePaul University	U.S. government (Department of Energy)	1995–2000	Egypt, Israel, and Jordan	Elimination of WMD

Table 2.1—Continued

Track Two Group	Primary Sponsor(s)	Period of Activity	Key Regional Participants' Countries of Origin	Discussion Topics
United Nations Institute for Disarmament Research	European governments, Sandia National Laboratories, U.S. Department of State	1993–present (last recorded Middle East meeting in 2003)	Arab states and Israel	Arms control handbook, commercial satellite and aerial imagery in arms control, technology related to verification
Cooperative Monitoring Center	Sandia National Laboratories	Early 1994–present	Arab states and Israel	Role of technology in confidence-building, verification exercises, border monitoring
Maritime activities	Canadian Government, U.S. Department of State	1995–2004	Arab states and Israel	Maritime safety colloquium for Middle East naval officers, maritime CBMs, SAR simulations
Regional Seismic Monitoring Cooperation Project	U.S. Geological Survey and Lawrence Livermore National Laboratory, U.S. Department of State	1992–present	Arab states and Israel	Database of Middle East seismic events, economic and urban regional planning, technology to monitor the CTBT
European activities	EU, OSCE, Wilton Park (British government), other European governments	Early 1990s to present	Arab states, Israel, Turkey, and Iran	Regional security charter, Mediterranean affairs, Arab-Israeli conflict, Iran

Table 2.1—Continued

Track Two Group	Primary Sponsor(s)	Period of Activity	Key Regional Participants' Countries of Origin	Discussion Topics
Gulf/2000	Columbia University and W. Alton Jones, Ford, MacArthur, Carnegie, Soros, and Exxon/Mobil Foundations	1993–present	Arab League states, Israel, Iran, and Turkey	Electronic network of Gulf specialists, conferences and workshops on Gulf-related topics, research resources on Gulf region
Stanley Foundation, with the Institute for Near East and Gulf Military Analyses	Stanley Foundation	2004–present	GCC states, Iran, Iraq, Yemen, other Middle East states	Alternative regional security frameworks for the Gulf
Gulf Weapons of Mass Destruction Free Zone	Gulf Research Center, Dubai—privately funded	2004–present	GCC states, Iran, Iraq, and Yemen	Creation of a WMDFZ in the Gulf

Through this process, a constituency supportive of regional cooperation emerges. This stage of track two activities has proved relatively
successful in the Middle East case and has produced more common
ideas and activities than many would have anticipated given the general breakdown of the Middle East peace process and the conflictual
regional environment following the Iraq war.

Because of the informal and off-the-record nature of track two
dialogues, the participants are provided an opportunity to engage
in frank discussion and explain the rationale for various policies (as
opposed to just repeating public rhetorical positions). Such opportunities for exchange can improve the parties' understanding of each
other's threat perceptions. For instance, one Gulf participant observed
that while he does not view Iran as a regional threat, security dialogues
have helped him understand why others do.[43] Gulf-oriented dialogues
have also sensitized American and other extraregional participants to
divisions and misperceptions among Arab Gulf states and Iran, and
have underscored the strong sense of nationalism among even more
progressive and Western-oriented Iranian participants (such as when
they take offense at the characterization of the subregion as the "Gulf"
as opposed to the "Persian Gulf").[44]

An Israeli participant similarly found value in learning about the
perceptions of the other side.[45] For example, before engaging in regional
security dialogues, the Israeli—a former general who has participated
in multiple track two activities, including those of UCLA, SIPRI, and
Search for Common Ground—was not aware of how others viewed
the balance of forces in the Middle East. Through the process, he
learned that the Arabs were aware of their weakness vis-à-vis Israel. He
explained how the Israelis always looked at quality *and* quantity and
thus thought the Arabs should be more confident because they have
more numbers. But the discussions convinced him that the Arabs feel
weak. This knowledge allowed the Israeli participant to better understand Arab sensitivities, leading him to become more cautious and sen-

---

[43] Interview with Omani participant, Muscat, Oman, September 24, 2000.

[44] Phone interview with Michael Kraig of the Stanley Foundation, November 28, 2006.

[45] Interview with Israeli analyst, Washington, D.C., November 30, 2000.

sitive to misperceptions and the importance of signals. Such under-standings also led to some concrete Israeli actions, such as its unilateral notification to its neighbors about large-scale exercises (including to the Syrians through the UN force in the Golan Heights).

The same Israeli participant also suggested that the better under-standing fostered through track two dialogues led Israel to become more receptive to certain arms control agreements, including the Chemical Weapons Convention (CWC) and the Convention on Certain Con-ventional Weapons (CCW). He also argued that such dialogue has affected Israeli thinking even in the sensitive area of nuclear weapons, leading to Israel's signing of the CTBT.[46] Of course, such dialogues do not change basic interests (e.g., Israel is unlikely to give up its nuclear capability), but the Israeli noted that they could create what he termed "a space of flexibility" within which contact can influence perceptions and (in a more limited way) policies.

Some Israeli participants also believe that understandings gen-erated through security dialogues influenced the positions of their Arab counterparts. For example, the Egyptian position in the arms control area has always been the most persistent, with the Egyptians insisting that regional arms control must focus on Israeli nuclear capa-bilities and Israeli adherence to the Nuclear Non-Proliferation Treaty (NPT) before tackling any broader issues. But the Israelis consistently explained to Egyptian participants that progress on the nuclear issue could not be made without Arab efforts to make Israel feel more secure, thus emphasizing the importance of incremental confidence-building. These Israelis felt that, because of such dialogues, Egyptian partici-pants now better understand the Israeli position on the nuclear issue and consequently may be more willing to discuss non-nuclear CBMs over time.

---

[46] Another Israeli participant familiar with regional arms control, however, does not believe that Israel signed the CTBT because of track two dialogue but rather because Israel had joined the Conference on Disarmament, so it wanted to be involved with the CTBT (interview with Israeli participant, Jerusalem, January 14, 2001). However, one may still ask whether partici-pation in such dialogues sensitized Israelis to the importance of global arms control, even if the dialogues themselves were not the sole trigger for specific policy outcomes.

Several other Israeli participants also shared examples relating to Israel's understanding of Iranian threat perceptions. One Israeli participant attended a meeting at which an Iranian academic with close contacts with Iranian officials presented a paper on Iranian threat perceptions.[47] As an Israeli, the participant was aware that Iran faced threats other than Israel, but he found it interesting how the Iranian differentiated between threat perceptions of the regime and those of the Iranian state itself. The presentation gave the Israeli insight into the evolutionary situation in internal Iranian politics and suggested to him that if ideological concerns recede and strategic concerns rise, common ground may be possible between Israel and Iran. An Israeli professor also noted that his contact with Iranians has increased his sensitivity to their threat perception of Israel and felt that their fears of Israeli attack sounded genuine.[48] As a consequence, his own views have changed with respect to Iran.

Another Israeli participant also noted the effect of track two dialogue on Israel's position toward Iran, arguing that Israel toned down its anti-Iranian rhetoric at that time.[49] He also believed that the Iranians were aware of these changes and were interested in engaging Israelis in substantive discussions to learn why Israelis behave as they do. For example, at one meeting, some Iranian participants were ignoring the Israeli participants at the more formal sessions, but during a break in the meeting the Iranians found the Israelis and engaged them in a substantive discussion on security issues. This Israeli participant also found that such dialogues gave him a better understanding not only of Iran but of the entire Gulf region. Another Israeli participant also found value in learning more about the domestic politics, constraints, and "unofficial public opinion" of Arab societies through such forums.[50] Track two dialogues not only help the parties understand the fundamental positions and policies of the other side, they also allow the

---

[47] Interview with Israeli official, Jerusalem, January 15, 2001.

[48] Interview with Israeli academic, Tel Aviv, January 18, 2001.

[49] Interview with Israeli analyst, Jerusalem, January 15, 2001.

[50] Interview with Israeli analyst, Tel Aviv, January 17, 2001.

exchange of views and perceptions on continuously evolving regional developments, a particularly important function during times of crisis, when misperceptions are likely to arise.[51]

Arab participants similarly pointed to examples suggesting the value of track two dialogue in sensitizing them to Israeli positions. One Jordanian participant noted how before such meetings, he did not believe that there were Israelis who genuinely wanted peace, and the sessions improved his understandings of Israeli perceptions.[52] Another Jordanian observed that he not only understood Israeli positions better (and also came to recognize that there were Israelis favoring compromise), but that such dialogues allowed him to affect Israeli thinking as well, leading Israeli participants to go home with better views of Jordan and to write favorable stories about Jordan in the press upon their return.[53]

An Egyptian participant observed how interactions with Israelis underscored for him how Israel faces problems similar to Egypt's (such as inadequate civilian control over the military), which normalized Israel in his mind and diminished the perception that Israel is invincible.[54] He also noted that track two contacts have allowed Israeli security analysts to appear on influential Egyptian television programs to explain Israeli positions. Moreover, this Egyptian analyst noted that he has changed his own language on radio or television programs since participating in track two dialogues, as he is more inclined to explain Israeli behavior rather than just blame Israel for its actions. Another Egyptian security analyst learned through such dialogues what was important to Israelis, which encouraged him to begin an Arab-Israeli peace movement among intellectuals.[55] This Egyptian analyst believed

---

[51] Interview with Israeli security analyst, Tel Aviv, January 17, 2001.

[52] Interview with Jordanian official, Amman, January 21, 2001.

[53] Interview with Jordanian security analyst, Amman, January 21, 2001.

[54] Interview with Egyptian military analyst, Cairo, January 22, 2001.

[55] Interview with Egyptian security analyst, Cairo, January 22, 2001.

that through track two dialogues, Israelis were better able to understand why Arabs feel threatened by Israel's nuclear capability.[56]

An additional aspect of the socialization stage is the building of knowledge and regional expertise in a particular issue area. Developing a shared sense of the problems faced by all parties and a common analytic framework by which to address them can give regional parties more confidence that a solution to their conflict is possible.

The Middle East regional security dialogues have produced numerous ideas for future regional security and arms control processes. The informal and academic atmosphere allows participants to engage in more creative, flexible, and long-term thinking than is possible in official forums. One example of this function was the SIPRI project that produced a document outlining guidelines for a future regional security regime. One prominent Egyptian participant believed that the SIPRI report had a major effect on regional thinking and that a future regional security structure after peace (i.e., after the conclusion of Arab-Israeli bilateral treaties) will depend largely on the ideas developed by such projects.[57] Indeed, several regional participants mentioned the SIPRI report as one of the most valuable products of track two activities. A U.S. State Department official also suggested that the SIPRI report was instrumental in shaping thinking at senior levels and encouraging senior officials to talk about post-peace issues and institutions more than they had in the past.[58] Many of the more practical projects in track two, such as cooperative maritime exercises and technology training, are also likely to lay the groundwork for future activities in an official Middle East arms control process.

Security dialogues have also educated regional elites about basic arms control concepts. For example, before such dialogues many regional participants—including prominent military and security

---

[56] One Egyptian participant and former high-level military official also noted the importance of such a forum for Egypt to tell the Israelis why it finds the nuclear issue so threatening; such communication cannot take place in an official, track one session (interview with Egyptian security analyst, Cairo, January 23, 2001).

[57] Interview with Egyptian security analyst, Cairo, January 22, 2001.

[58] Interview with U.S. official, Washington, D.C., November 21, 2000.

analysts—were not familiar with concepts such as CBMs or the arms control experiences of other regions. Many of the early track two meetings focused explicitly on seminars led by extraregional participants about the arms control experiences in their regions in order to draw lessons for the Middle East and introduce an arms control vocabulary to the region. Projects such as UNIDIR's arms control handbooks have contributed to building a common knowledge base on regional arms control. Regional elites have also become familiar with technology needed for verification of arms control agreements through training courses provided by track two sponsors. The development of technology for mutual verification monitoring can be useful for future peace agreements.[59] Taken together, these track two activities have developed a cadre of thousands of regional elites who are now familiar with regional arms control issues on both the analytic and operational level. Such common knowledge will help ensure that when an official arms control process begins again, it will not resume in a vacuum.[60]

Finally, during the socialization stage, many participants in security dialogues begin to identify themselves as part of a distinct group. To be sure, national identities never recede and sometimes are reinforced through such processes. But, over time, some participants feel that they belong to a group that thinks differently from those who are outside the process. The author's personal observation of track two activity, including of a small group session during which track two participants explicitly discussed the value and role of track two diplomacy, underscored this dynamic, with many of the participants speaking of the process as if it were a club that needed to be preserved and strengthened.

Several participants noted that they find it easier to talk to other track two group members even if the context is not a track two setting. All track two participants are also in the "same boat" in terms of justi-

---

[59] An Egyptian participant believed that such technology should be developed so that it is ready when the political environment improves and peace treaties have been established (interview with Egyptian security analyst, Cairo, January 23, 2001).

[60] An Egyptian official viewed this aspect of track two as one of its more valuable contributions, especially since no formal process has operated since 1995 (interview with Egyptian official, Cairo, January 22, 2001).

fying what they do when they go back home.[61] One track two participant in the maritime colloquium exercise observed that the dialogues and exercises over time have helped the participants develop a feeling of common interest.[62] Whether such a sense of common interest can spread beyond the select group of participating elites is a challenge for many track two exercises.

Filtering

Security-related dialogues in the Middle East have not been terribly successful in moving beyond socializing the participating elites and toward filtering the resulting concepts and understandings to broader segments of society. Many of the issues discussed in such dialogues are still too sensitive to be included in public discourse, particularly in the current regional environment. The combination of a deadlocked Middle East peace process and the bloody and uncertain aftermath of the Iraq war make regional discussions of confidence-building and cooperative security difficult. And even when the regional environment was more favorable, such as in the mid-1990s following the Oslo breakthrough, ideas and papers discussed in track two circles did not receive wide attention, because organizers of such groups rightly worried that publicity would undermine the ability of the groups to continue their work. Both Arab and Israeli participants were cautious about preventing results of group discussions from leaking into the public domain, making the ability to disseminate their ideas extremely difficult.

Some joint regional publications emerged from track two projects, but such studies were narrowly distributed and did not create new regional discussions like those generated by the 1993 publication of Shimon Peres and Arye Naor's book *The New Middle East* (which called for greater regional cooperation but actually led to a backlash in the Arab world as it was perceived as an attempt to exert Israeli hegemony over the region). Individual participants on occasion did provide insights from their track two discussions during media interviews, but such expressions have been too isolated and infrequent to have a

---

[61] Interview with Israeli analyst, Tel Aviv, January 17, 2001.

[62] Interview with Israeli official, Tel Aviv, January 16, 2001.

strong and coherent regional impact. Moreover, Middle East security dialogues have not broadened sufficiently to constituencies beyond a core group of security elites, such as to journalists, parliamentarians, or youth (some individuals from these sectors participate in such dialogues, but there is no track two dialogue devoted entirely to reaching out to them). The Middle East also still lacks regional centers focused on regional security issues, although some attempts have been made in this direction.[63] The CMC in Amman is a rare example of a regional security center initiated from within the region—albeit with significant support from the CMC at Sandia—and an attempt to spread cooperative security ideas and training to the broader region.

The Egyptian-sponsored trilateral (Egyptian, Israeli, and Jordanian) arms control project was another example of an indigenous track two effort—but under the umbrella of an Egyptian-born law professor in the United States. While this group included influential members of strategic studies institutes in each respective country and thus had the potential to create regional institutional links, the group quickly raised suspicions and resistance among Israeli officials. The Israelis believed that the Egyptians were using the forum as a way to "drive a wedge between Israeli academics and their government" on the nuclear issue, which undermined the legitimacy of the groups' work in terms of its ability to present a neutral forum for dialogue on regional security.[64] The participation of only three regional actors also limited the ability of the group to create a broader regional forum for security dialogue. And like other track two efforts in the region, the groups' deliberations were private and not widely accessible.

Other indigenous track two efforts have emerged in the Gulf, such as the initiative to create a GWMDFZ. But such groups are, by defini-

---

[63] The official ACRS process established a regional security center in Amman, but due to the breakdown of the official process and the general regional tension, the center was unable to begin functioning as planned. A U.S. university sponsored a project to create an Association of National Security Centers, but such efforts have fallen short of the creation of a regional center focusing on security issues as exists in South Asia.

[64] Agha et al. (2003, p. 131). According to this source, the Israeli government was so disturbed by this group that it tried to convince the U.S. government to stop funding the project.

tion, limited to the Gulf subregion and thus do not provide a forum for broader and regularized Arab-Israeli security dialogue. Although government officials are familiar with these groups' work, it is unclear whether Arab publics are familiar with their existence and the concepts discussed and promoted through this process. Finally, discussion of nuclear capabilities and their implications on a regionwide basis, as occurs in South Asia, is still a taboo subject in key countries such as Israel.

In short, ideas supporting regional security cooperation are still unknown or unpopular in the Middle East. That said, more recent and limited track two dialogues (such as those focusing on Gulf security) have made more concerted efforts to reach larger audiences by spreading their ideas through various media outlets. Whether such ideas will ever influence or shape official policy is still unknown, but such groups are attempting to avoid the politicized aspects of Arab-Israeli relations and build common security thinking around other regional concepts.

Policy Impact

It is difficult to measure policy influence and demonstrate that a particular policy outcome originated in ideas produced in a track two venue, although with process tracing and participant interviews some examples emerge.[65] Because many Arab and Israeli track two participants are influential elites with connections to official decisionmakers (if they are not decisionmakers themselves), track two efforts are on occasion well known among governments in the region, sometimes at high levels.[66]

For example, the first IGCC track two workshop on the Middle East took place 10 days after the Iraqi invasion of Kuwait in 1990, and

---

[65] For example, both the original Oslo negotiations and the Sturmont negotiations in Northern Ireland started with track two meetings, and a good part of the final agreement in Northern Ireland was actually hammered out in such meetings.

[66] For example, one Jordanian participant claimed that he had given briefings on track two meetings to up to 50 Jordanian officials (interview with Jordanian security analyst, Amman, January 21, 2001). Israeli participants in regional security track two dialogues also have strong connections to senior government officials (see, for example, Agha et al., 2003, p. 129).

the second convened a week before the Arab-Israeli Madrid peace conference in October 1991. Since many of the same regional elites left the
IGCC conference to attend the formal Madrid talks, some considered
the track two conference a "trial run." Moreover, ideas developed in
the IGCC workshops covering multilateral issue areas influenced the
official ACRS Working Group as well as the economic components of
the Israeli-Palestinian Oslo process, according to participants in the
process.

The development of personal relationships can also lead to some
limited spillover to official policy. For example, one Israeli participant
associated with the Likud party used his track two contacts with Jordanian counterparts to arrange meetings between Benjamin Netanyahu
(before he became prime minister of Israel) and Jordanian officials,
including then–Crown Prince Hassan.[67] An Israeli participant also
noted how personal contacts established in track two groups allowed
members of the top political echelon to pass messages or to clarify
points, particularly with respect to the Palestinian track.[68]

Personal contacts among officials participating in track two (always
in an unofficial capacity) can also prove useful when the officials meet
in non–track two settings. Because an Israeli knew an Egyptian coun-
terpart from track two meetings, he found it easier to negotiate with
him at the official level when the two were working on language for a
global arms control agreement.[69] There is also evidence that ideas from
track two projects can affect thinking and policy statements at the
highest levels of government. For example, after learning of efforts to
establish a regional security regime from well-connected participants in
the DePaul track two project, Foreign Minister Amr Moussa of Egypt
gave a speech before the UN General Assembly in 1997 discussing the
regional security regime concept.[70]

---

[67] Interview with American analyst, Washington, D.C., January 11, 2001, and interview
with American analyst, Amman, January 21, 2001.

[68] Interview with Israeli analyst, Jerusalem, January 15, 2001.

[69] Interview with Israeli official, Jerusalem, January 15, 2001.

[70] Interview with American participant, Chicago, February 22, 2001.

Even some limited impact on the bilateral tracks is evident. One Jordanian participant who conducted a joint study with an Israeli in a track two group on Israeli-Jordanian security issues suggested that this document affected how senior-level Jordanian officials (including the former king) thought about the Israeli side and ultimately influenced the security section of the Israel-Jordan peace treaty.[71] In the Search for Common Ground case, track two participants deliberately tried to produce a breakthrough in the Israeli-Syrian bilateral track, although the effort failed. But such deliberate attempts to influence the bilateral tracks are rare in multilateral security dialogues, which usually involve a much broader and more regional focus. In this sense, its greatest impact on policy will probably be apparent when an official regional arms control process reemerges.

In the Gulf arena, the GRC's efforts to forward the idea of a GWMDFZ have reached official deliberations within the GCC and the Arab League, prompting heated exchanges between the two Arab institutions. Indeed, the initiative is viewed by some as a challenge to the Arab order, seeking to promote subregional arrangements without regard for traditional Arab leaders such as Egypt or traditional rivals such as Israel. While the region may be many years away from the establishment of such a zone, the discussions on this issue have affected regional thinking and discourse about the future of regional security and inter-Arab relations.

The Gulf dialogues promoted by the Stanley Foundation also seem to be having an effect on the thinking of key regional policy-makers. For example, a former senior Iranian official presented a talk at a track two meeting in Tehran in the fall of 2006 suggesting the need to move the regional security system beyond *realpolitik* and security based on balances of power and hegemony toward a more coop-erative arrangement, directly mirroring many of the ideas presented through the Stanley Foundation's publications based on its track two workshops.[72]

---

[71]   Interview with Jordanian security analyst, Amman, January 21, 2001.

[72]   Phone interview with Michael Kraig of the Stanley Foundation, November 28, 2006.

Gulf/2000 discussions also regularly spark debate and ideas that may be taken up in official circles over time. For example, Gulf/2000 held a conference on the future of Iraq in July 2000 that brought together a group of U.S. State Department officials and exiled Iraqis to produce a series of studies considering Iraq after Saddam Hussein.[73] Many of these same individuals later worked together in the official "Future of Iraq" project sponsored by the U.S. State Department from October 2001 to the spring of 2003.[74] The State Department official who ran the project, Thomas S. Warrick, attended the Gulf/2000 Cyprus meeting.

Limits

Elites

Many of the limitations discussed earlier have emerged as problems in the Middle East case, including the participation of ideological elites leading to tense deliberations. At one meeting, a particularly heated exchange between an Israeli and Egyptian on the nuclear issue left a negative impression with an Israeli participant, who began to question the value of such activity and felt that such exchanges only hardened positions.[75] Another Israeli participant similarly observed that the tense Israeli-Egyptian dynamic at the meetings led him to view the Egyptians more negatively, remarking that it appeared as if the Iranians and Syrians were more capable of "civilized" dialogue with the Israelis than were the Egyptians. He felt that some (though not all) Egyptians were relaying official government positions and "toeing the line" rather than engaging in serious dialogue. In a different meeting, one Israeli found that an encounter with a Syrian only underscored how far apart the parties were and convinced him that the gaps were unbridgeable,

---

[73] The findings of the meeting were published in *Middle East Policy* (2000).

[74] Email correspondence with Gary Sick, September 12, 2006, and Lawrence Potter, September 13, 2006.

[75] Interview with Israeli academic, Jerusalem, January 14, 2001.

a view he did not hold going into the process.[76] Arab parties similarly have expressed concern about hardliners on the Israeli side, noting how participation of ideological rather than pragmatic individuals can undermine the process.

Another common problem with track two in the Middle East is the potential for misinformation. Although participants are not speaking at the official level, at times the positions they suggest that their government will take do not accurately portray official position.[77] One Israeli participant expressed concern that some Israelis have at times indicated concessions that were perceived by Arab interlocutors to suggest a margin of flexibility when such flexibility did not exist, such as on the nuclear issue.[78]

Domestic Constraints

Domestic environments, particularly in the Arab world, make participants cautious about exposing track two ideas to wider audiences. Cooperation with Israel is a dangerous endeavor in many Arab states and certainly in Iran. Public opinion in the Arab world is wary of normalization with Israel, even in countries such as Egypt and Jordan, which have signed peace treaties with Israel. Indeed, the gap between governmental acceptance of Israel and public acceptance is wide; professional societies across the Arab world ban their members from contact with Israelis even when governmental contacts are taking place. And Israelis are also wary of multilateral cooperative efforts that are viewed as potential forums for other nations to "gang up" and pressure Israel.

Such sensitivities help explain why media exposure often impedes such dialogues.[79] Although track two dialogues are not secret, they

---

[76] Interview with Israeli official, Tel Aviv, January 18, 2001.

[77] A senior Israeli official expressed this concern in an interview with the author in Washington, D.C., on April 11, 2001.

[78] Interview with Israeli analyst, Jerusalem, January 15, 2001.

[79] Other studies of unofficial dialogues have also demonstrated that increased publicity can lead to greater posturing and rigidity and a reduced likelihood that talks will occur at all. The Oslo negotiations are a case in point. Elaborate efforts were made to keep these secret,

are kept low-profile, and the sponsors guarantee the confidentiality of the participants. Consequently, exposure of particular participants can prove embarrassing and damaging to individuals' careers (and in some cases can even risk the physical safety of participants), jeopardizing the process as a whole. Some governments, such as Syria's, are extremely suspicious of track two activity and very rarely give the green light for individuals to participate. The Syrians fear that informal contacts are dangerous and that the Israelis may use them to embarrass Syria by revealing that it is "flexible" and willing to hold "secret talks."[80] As with other regional cooperative initiatives, the Syrians view such contacts as a concession to Israel absent a peace treaty between the two countries.

Two instances of leaks to the media exemplify the negative impact of media exposure. The first occurred in the Search for Common Ground's working group in 1994, when discussions between Israelis and Syrians regarding security arrangements were leaked to the press (Ya'ari, 1994, Olster, 1994, and "Syrian, Israeli Academics Met Secretly in Oslo," 1994). Some suspect that the source of the leak was an Israeli opposed to the types of concessions being discussed in the talks in an effort to sabotage the process, although the Palestinians also used the leak to embarrass the Syrians.[81] It worked. The Syrians immediately pulled out of the process. Another leak to the press occurred in one of the UCLA sessions in Cairo in July 2000, with an article listing the names of the Iranian, Syrian, Lebanese, Israeli, and American participants. This time, an Egyptian was suspected as the source of the leak. As a result, a Syrian participant was warned not to attend such meetings again.[82] The Iranians who attended this meeting faced professional pressures upon their return and did not attend future track two talks.

Domestic sensitivities are also apparent in Gulf track two efforts, where the tendency to avoid the Israeli-Palestinian conflict can be used

---

because they otherwise could not have taken place (Pruitt, 1997, p. 246). In addition, had the informal, mediated dialogue between Sinn Fein and the British government that led to the Sturmont talks been publicized, it could not have continued (Pruitt, 2000).

[80] Interview with American analyst, Washington, D.C., January 11, 2001.

[81] Interview with Jordanian security analyst, Amman, January 21, 2001.

[82] Interview with U.S. official, Washington, D.C., November 21, 2000.

by Arab actors opposed to such efforts to embarrass Gulf states and question their Arab credentials. Indeed, at the official level, the GCC states are still under pressure to follow a pan-Arab line and focus on Israel, as reflected in the December 2005 GCC summit final statement in which "urged by Amr Moussa, the Secretary General of the Arab League, they agreed to condemn Israel's nuclear arsenal" while failing to mention Iranian nuclear activities and violations (El-Hokayem and Legrenzi, 2006, p. 8). GRC's efforts faced similar resistance from Arab League Secretary-General Moussa. Such sensitivity demonstrates the difficulties the Gulf track two efforts will face in moving their ideas into official decisionmaking circles and gaining broader legitimacy.

The Regional Environment
Violent regional episodes have impeded progress on many occasions. It is an irony of track two dialogues that when they are most needed, it is difficult to bring them about. This is because in a tense regional environment, regional sensitivities make it challenging to establish and maintain dialogue. Because track two dialogue is unofficial, it has been better able than official regional processes to insulate itself from the political environment, but not completely. This is particularly the case for Arab and Iranian participants, whose governments often provide signals suggesting whether they approve of their participation in such forums. Some governments may be less willing to allow their nationals to participate in such activities in the midst of negative regional developments.

Several track two activities planned for the fall of 2000, for example, were postponed due to violence between Israelis and Palestinians following the al-Aksa intifada. The danger of track two processes being held captive to political developments at the official track is very real. Although many track two dialogues continued despite the violence and deadlock in the Middle East peace process, and new ones have emerged in the Gulf, there is no doubt that a more favorable regional environment—particularly a resolution to the Israeli-Palestinian conflict and stability in Iraq—would improve the prospects for track two diplomacy across the region.

Conclusion

Despite significant limitations, track two diplomacy in the Middle East has proven an important mechanism to improve communication among regional actors and build regional understanding and knowledge in the arms control and regional security realm. Its socialization function has led a core and not-insignificant number of security elites across the region to begin thinking and speaking in similar ways. And promising new efforts have sprung up in the Gulf region in recent years, leading to new regional security communities increasingly thinking in cooperative terms.

However, without these elites going back to their own societies and spreading such ideas and knowledge (i.e., developing a broader constituency supportive of regional arms control and cooperative security concepts), the impact on national and regional policy is likely to be minimal. As the Soviet experience demonstrates, track two ideas can influence official thinking even in authoritarian systems. But future work should consider whether effecting policy change might be easier in democratic environments, where filtering track two ideas to broader domestic constituencies may increase pressure for policy change.

High-profile official policymakers willing to promote arms control and regional security concepts among key Arab and Israeli constituencies would also boost the prospects for track two ideas to influence policy, but such ideas also must have regional legitimacy. This requires more open and broader public discussions of track two security ideas despite the drawbacks of exposure. Naturally, some regional security concepts will be too technical and mundane to generate the broad regional discussion that surrounds issues such as Iraq or democracy in the Middle East. But debate about the general concept of a regional security structure based on a cooperative rather than competitive security premise (and the related discussion of regional military budgets and arms racing versus development needs) is conceivable, particularly given the high level of regional interest in the Iranian nuclear dispute. With more open debate on contentious regional issues developing throughout the Arab world through growing satellite television networks, discussion of new cooperative regional security structures among a broad audience is within reach. Such discussion would enable the knowledge accumulated from over 15 years of security dialogues to reach vast audiences and potentially have a much deeper impact on national and regional security policy in the future.

CHAPTER THREE

Regional Security Dialogues in South Asia

Introduction

As in the Middle East, South Asia experienced the growth of track two dialogues in the 1990s, many of which focused on security-related issues. One survey found that by 1996, more than 40 nonofficial dialogues were operating within South Asia and that another dozen were taking place outside the region with regular regional participation (Behera, Evans, and Rizvi, 1997, p. 4). The end of the Cold War and the uncertain role of extraregional actors (in conjunction with the rise of neighboring China) led to greater regional interest and activism in addressing a multitude of regional conflicts and challenges. Because the central official regional institution, SAARC, has avoided contentious bilateral disputes and political issues, some regional actors turned to unofficial dialogues to fill the gap.

The South Asian region is traditionally defined through the regional members of SAARC: India, Pakistan, Bangladesh, Sri Lanka, Nepal, Bhutan, the Maldives, and, as of December 2005, Afghanistan. However, a number of areas of contention—water disputes, insurgencies, tribal associations, organized criminal networks, and ethnic tensions—span national borders and overlap with other regions (particularly Central Asia), contributing to a complex and turbulent regional environment.[1]

---

[1] For the complex and overlapping security relationships in the broader region, see Peters et al. (2006, especially Chapter Three).

One of the most serious regional challenges is the Indian-Pakistani dispute over Kashmir, the most central regional conflict and a barrier to normalization and broader conflict resolution in the region. India and Pakistan have fought three wars since their partition in 1947 following British rule, two of them over Kashmir (an additional interstate war between India and China occurred in 1962). The Line of Control (LOC) dividing Kashmir into Indian- and Pakistani-controlled areas is a continued source of tension and instability, with the crisis in 2001–2002 leading to nearly a million troops facing off along the border for almost a year after India claimed that Pakistan was responsible for terrorist attacks in its territory.[2] This territorial dispute is particularly dangerous, as it has been infused with religious ideology: Some Islamic militants view the conflict as a jihad, energizing an already-growing Hindu nationalist movement in India. Periodic official peace efforts for nearly 60 years—including the process starting in January 2004—have not yet succeeded in resolving this dispute.[3] The breakdown of previous peace initiatives due to violent crises, such as the Kargil conflict in the spring of 1999 that put an end to the Lahore Peace Process, have further undermined confidence that a peace agreement is possible.

Indeed, some analysts are skeptical of a complete resolution of Kashmir and predict future deadlock given the fundamental asymmetries of interest on this issue (India prefers the status quo, while Pakistan rejects the existing LOC as the international border) and the fact that Pakistan would have to completely dismantle an expansive militant infrastructure (United States Institute of Peace, 2005). Moreover, Kashmir is a particularly difficult dispute to resolve because the conflict is as much about identity as it is about territory (Schaffer and Schaffer, 2005). The fact that India and Pakistan have, since their 1998 nuclear tests, openly declared their nuclear weapon status has exacerbated an already tense situation, as has continued regional arms racing and large defense expenditures. In such an environment, unofficial dia-

---

[2]   United States Institute of Peace (2005). For a discussion of the causes and evolution of the Kashmir conflict, see Schaffer and Schaffer (2005).

[3]   On recent peace initiatives, see Schaffer (2005a) and Lancaster (2005).

logues can prove particularly beneficial by offering fresh ideas that can reshape regional thinking and policy on this difficult problem.

In addition to the core conflict between India and Pakistan, the region also faces a variety of other regional disputes and challenges. These include the Ganges water dispute between India and Bangladesh, India's role in Sri Lanka and its relationship to the Tamil Tigers, and tensions between India and its other, smaller regional neighbors such as the Maldives and Bhutan. Nepal's relationship with China as a means to balance India's regional ambitions also adds complexity to the regional environment, as do India's larger security postures and perceptions of Chinese power (which also influence discussions of regional arms control). Pakistan's unstable border with Afghanistan and internal instability further contribute to this volatile regional security environment, as does the internal instability of other South Asian actors facing antistate forces. Such political and security challenges, in addition to development dilemmas and regional export markets, lead to the additional problem of low intraregional trade and economic cooperation. Indeed, many track two dialogues are trying to improve this situation by creating a sense of South Asian identity, fostering greater regional cooperation in the political, security, and economic areas.

Creating a sense of regional identity and a culture of cooperation is a significant challenge in a region with little tradition of either. The evidence to date suggests that the direct influence of such dialogues on official policy has been minimal, although not entirely absent. South Asian dialogues have had some success in building a constituency supportive of South Asian cooperation, including in challenging areas such as nuclear confidence-building. South Asia has also proven more successful than the Middle East in filtering track two ideas to wider audiences, improving their prospects for influencing official political processes under ripe conditions and increasing the legitimacy of such ideas. Although South Asian track two dialogues have faced limitations similar to those of Middle East track two efforts, the outlook for South Asian track two appears more promising at this time.[4]

---

[4] In the 1990s, there were some South Asians who viewed the situation in reverse, believing that progress in the Arab-Israeli peace process suggested that South Asia should learn les-

Overview of Dialogues

The following review of South Asian dialogues focuses on several of the most prominent security-related processes that fit this study's definition of track two in order to illustrate the type of activity occurring in the region.[5] While many unofficial dialogues initially focused more on regional economic and development issues, track two dialogues have become increasingly political since the 1990s (Waslekar, 1995), with several focusing explicitly on core political and security issues, including nuclear weapon proliferation and the status of Kashmir. One project sponsored by the International Peace Academy, for example, sought to find new voices from Pakistan, India, and Kashmir among a younger generation of scholars to exchange ideas and develop different approaches to resolving this conflict, an effort that produced an edited volume authored by regional participants.[6]

As in the case of the Middle East, most track two dialogues are conducted in English and are organized and funded by sources from outside the region, leading to similar perceptions of external imposition. One regional observer suggests that the U.S. government and private institutions were initially focused on bringing influential South Asians together to create a nuclear restraint regime, but the substance of track two discussion broadened, as "it was soon realized that the nuclear issue in South Asia could not be separated from other elements in India-Pakistan relations, such as the conventional arms race, Kashmir, and economic development" (Waslekar, 1995, p. 5).

---

sons from the Middle East for its own conflict-resolution efforts. For such explorations, see Ahmar (2001).

[5]   For a detailed list of a broader range of unofficial dialogues, see Behera, Evans, and Rizvi (1997, pp. 51–98). This inventory is broader than track two dialogues closely connected to government officials or policy-oriented think tanks and includes a variety of other unofficial regional activity, including civil society groups, business networks, grassroots people-to-people networks, and activities outside the region that bring South Asians together. Also see Behera (2002).

[6]   Sidhu, Asif, and Samii, eds. (2006). Two prominent Indian and Pakistani scholars, P. R. Chari and Hasan Askari-Rizvi, assisted the International Peace Academy in identifying young scholars to engage in dialogue and research on this issue.

Participants in such dialogues are largely academics, retired military and civilian officials, journalists, and NGO representatives, with some involvement from the business sector (see Behera, Evans, and Rizvi, 1997, p. 26). Some track two dialogues also involve government officials acting in an unofficial capacity, sometimes referred to as "observers."

Neemrana Process

This Indian-Pakistani initiative, which has been largely financed by the U.S. government and the Ford Foundation, began in 1991, serving as a forum for academics and former diplomats and military officials to discuss contentious security issues (including Kashmir and nuclear questions). The model for the group is the Dartmouth Process, used in the U.S.-Soviet dialogues, and involves bringing influential elites together to lay the groundwork for major shifts in security thinking and policy. The group has presented a joint policy paper on options for Kashmir to the Indian and Pakistani governments and a variety of other reports on Kashmir and nuclear issues.[7] Although the governments of India and Pakistan are not involved in the process, they have facilitated the dialogue by granting visas to participants on a priority basis (Waslekar, 1995, p. 6). The participants selected have also been influential elites: Two of the Pakistani members are known to be influential in the military, and another Pakistani participant was considered for the interim prime ministership in the transition government in 1993; participants also include a retired Indian general and admiral and former civilian officials (Waslekar, 1995, p. 6). However, according to Ambassador Teresita Schaffer, director of the South Asia Program at the Center for Strategic and International Studies (CSIS), the process began to "run out of steam" by the mid-1990s as returning participants who briefed officials back home tended to defer to traditional government positions.[8] Despite occasional opinion pieces by group participants in local

---

[7] For a summary of the Neemrana process and similar track two processes, see Notter and McDonald (1996).

[8] Interview with Teresita Schaffer, Washington, D.C., January 16, 2002.

media reflecting the thinking of the track two discussions, the group has not had a measurable policy impact on government officials.[9]

Balusa Group

In 1995, Shirin Tahir-Kheli (a professor at Johns Hopkins University who would later serve in a number of senior governmental posts in President George W. Bush's first and second administrations) and her brother, Toufiq Siddiqi (an environmental and energy expert), established the Balusa Group to discuss ways to improve the Indian-Pakistani relationship.[10] With funding from the UN Development Programme and the Rockefeller Foundation, the group brought together a high-profile group of Indian and Pakistani generals, policymakers, and academics to discuss ideas for building confidence between the two neighbors and for resolving contentious issues such as Kashmir (Dixit, 2005). More generally, the group sought to broaden definitions of security beyond narrow military strategic calculations to areas such as economic and energy cooperation (see, for example, Kheli, 1997). The group has met on a continual basis since its first meeting in Singapore.

One of the more prominent projects emerging from the group was the idea for a joint pipeline to pump natural gas from Iran to India and Pakistan, addressing the growing energy needs of the two countries while also serving as a peace-building exercise. The group studied the energy needs of India and Pakistan and sponsored a technical team that proposed the project.[11] As Siddiqi explained in an interview about the origins of the group, "Shirin and I have had a continuous interest in promoting sustainable development in the Subcontinent, and here was a concept [the pipeline proposal] that would represent a win-win economic situation for the key adversaries, while also serving as a CBM" (Dixit, 2005).

---

[9]   Interview with Teresita Schaffer, Washington, D.C., January 16, 2002.

[10]   Both Tahir-Kheli and Siddiqi spent part of their childhood in Pakistan before their family immigrated to the United States. See Dixit (2005).

[11]   The project is discussed in Durrani (2001, p. 74).

Another founding member of the group, retired general Mahmud Ali Durrani (currently serving as Pakistani ambassador to the United States), also strongly supported the project for peace-building purposes, arguing, "The peace dividend will begin to flow the moment you sign the document. There will be newfound confidence as you move into detailed studies, construction, the to-and-fro between officials, and so on" (Dixit, 2005). Some argue that in addition to creating more economic stakeholders supporting Indian-Pakistani peace efforts, the pipeline project could also help address the Kashmir conflict by de-prioritizing the issue and changing mind-sets.[12] After the emergence of the official composite dialogue between India and Pakistan, this project received a boost and moved from track two discussions to the official track one level.[13]

On Kashmir, the group has sought to question the notion of sovereignty and generate new thinking on potential solutions. The group also produced a paper on cooperative monitoring and the role of technology in India-Pakistan agreements that was supported by the Sandia National Laboratories, the sponsor of a cooperative monitoring center starting in 1994 that has hosted track two activities in both the Middle East and South Asia.[14] General Durrani produced a monograph outlining the costs of war for India and Pakistan and the benefits of a more cooperative relationship based on concepts discussed by the Balusa Group (Durrani, 2001). According to Teresita Schaffer, despite the limited influence of the group in official policy circles, some participants (including General Durrani) have been pushing this new thinking with colleagues in the Pakistani defense ministry.[15]

The Balusa Group also reflects the role of track two processes in keeping dialogue channels open even during tense regional periods, such as when the group met in Lahore in the fall of 1999 in the wake of

---

[12] See quotes from Indian scholars and others in the "Mother of All CBMs" section in Dixit (2005).

[13] For details of the proposal and official opposition from Washington, see Fatah (2005).

[14] See Sandia National Laboratories (2004) for a comprehensive description of the work of the CMCs in both South Asia and the Middle East.

[15] Interview with Teresita Schaffer, Washington, D.C., January 16, 2002.

the military coup in Pakistan to discuss and analyze the Kargil conflict (Durrani, 2001, p. 68).

Kashmir Study Group (KSG)

In 1996 the U.S.-based KSG formed among a group of academics, former officials, NGO leaders, and legislators—mostly from the United States, Canada, and Europe—to advance a peaceful, practical, and honorable solution to the Kashmir problem.[16] M. Farooq Kathwari, a Kashmiri-American businessman, founded the KSG and funded the project. According to two South Asia observers, the KSG "has achieved a reputation for nonpartisan objectivity that has earned it a hearing in New Delhi and Islamabad, and a measure of confidence among Kashmiri leaders" (Schaffer and Schaffer, 2005, p. 313).

In 1999 the KSG hosted a small group of retired Indian and Pakistani officials who produced a report in 2000, "Kashmir: A Way Forward" (Kashmir Study Group, 2000) which described a novel potential approach to creating a special status for Kashmir (recommending that a portion of Kashmir be developed into two sovereign entities but without an international status).[17] Similar ideas for moving ahead in Kashmir were produced in a second 2005 report based on discussions at a Pugwash conference with participants from different parts of Kashmir (Kashmir Study Group, 2005). The group's ambition is that the ideas produced in these reports will shape future peace proposals on the subject. The KSG also sponsors longer background reports, such as one on the Kashmir conflict after 50 years[18] and another on the economics of peacemaking in Kashmir (Schaffer, 2005b).

Shanghai Process

Meetings for this initiative began in 1994 and included twenty-five high-level participants from China, India, Pakistan, and the United

---

[16] Email correspondence with Teresita Schaffer, June 1, 2006. For KSG's statement of purpose, see its Web site, as of June 15, 2007:
http://www.kashmirstudygroup.net/

[17] For details, see Schaffer and Schaffer (2005, p. 313). Both authors are KSG members.

[18] Forthcoming on the KSG Web site.

States.[19] Although India and Pakistan generally did not send government officials to the meetings, government officials have represented China and the United States in an unofficial capacity.[20] According to one American participant, the early meetings of the group did not go well; the participants tended to be ideological and nationalistic, and it was difficult to find regional participants who were willing to think more broadly.[21] At a meeting in Washington, D.C., in 2000, the participants began to display more openness to new ideas, but the American observer noted that, by this point, the group's participants did not have influence within their respective governments, a common dilemma for many track two efforts.[22]

Areas of discussion for the group included domestic and foreign policy constraints in the participating countries, the global and regional context for reducing the political and military need for nuclear weapons, fissile material production cut-off, ballistic missile proliferation (including a proposal for a ballistic missile freeze in the region), and no-first-use security assurances (Behera, Evans, and Rizvi, 1997, p. 92). However, despite agreements regarding ballistic missile issues, the proposals ultimately did not move forward because of the limited influence of the individuals involved in the process.[23] This process also avoided publicity and was sensitive to media exposure after several participants leaked agreements from the talks in the early meetings, raising larger questions about its ability to influence broader public and official opinion given the confidential nature of the discussions.[24]

Stimson Center Dialogues

Since 1991, the Henry L. Stimson Center in Washington, D.C., has been training Indian, Pakistani, and Chinese officials, military person-

---

[19] For a partial list of participant names, see Behera (1997, p. 92).

[20] Interview with U.S. State Department official, Washington, D.C., July 1, 2002.

[21] Interview with U.S. State Department official, Washington, D.C., July 1, 2002.

[22] Interview with U.S. State Department official, Washington, D.C., July 1, 2002.

[23] Interview with U.S. State Department official, Washington, D.C., July 1, 2002.

[24] Interview with U.S. State Department official, Washington, D.C., July 1, 2002.

nel, academics, and journalists on issues of regional confidence-building and arms control. The objectives of its South Asia programming include stabilizing and reducing the dangers of nuclear weapons in the region, facilitating movement on the Kashmir conflict, and promoting regional stability and normalization between India and Pakistan (Krepon and Haider, 2004). The center regularly convenes track two workshops on nuclear risk reduction and escalation control and runs a visiting fellows program that has hosted more than 65 Pakistani and Indian journalists, academics, researchers, and military officers in an effort to increase mutual understanding and promote problem-solving analysis.

A major report resulting from the center's activities suggests specific recommendations for nuclear risk reduction that it claims, in the current political environment, are "now ripe for official consideration" (see Laipson, 2004). The premise of the report is the need to supplement unilateral initiatives to reduce nuclear dangers (including such scenarios as a nuclear incident or the use of a dirty bomb by a terrorist group) with cooperative measures, emphasizing cooperative security themes common in many track two security dialogues. Other Stimson Center reports present national perspectives and solutions to regional security problems, such as one by Pakistani analyst Zawar Haider Abidi explaining his nation's perception of its nuclear capability (as a deterrent and balance to India's conventional military advantage) and its subsequent rejection of no–first use policy given its perceived vulnerability to Indian conventional forces (Abidi, 2003). Abidi suggests that, because of such perceptions, Pakistan's offensive nuclear posture is unlikely to change without shifts in the conventional balance of forces, requiring CBMs to demonstrate nonhostile intent (e.g., halting training along the LOC in Kashmir or the prenotification of major military exercises).

A number of CBMs advocated and nurtured through the Stimson dialogues have also been implemented at official levels, such as the ballistic missile flight test notification agreement, military exercise notifications and constraint measures along international borders, and

Kashmir-related CBMs.[25] Stimson organizers also believe that their workshops and publications on nuclear terrorism have raised considerable consciousness of this problem in official circles, particularly since the September 11, 2001, attacks on the United States.[26]

CSIS Meetings on Nuclear Risk Reduction Centres (NRRCs)

From December 2003 to May 2004, CSIS, a Washington-based nonpartisan think tank, organized three workshops in the United Kingdom (with support from the Nuclear Threat Initiative, an NGO working in the counterproliferation area) to consider nuclear risk reduction measures in South Asia. Robert Einhorn, a former senior U.S. official with significant expertise in non-proliferation, led the project. The model for the project was the NRRCs that were established by the United States and Soviet Union during the Cold War.

The workshops included a group of 17 senior nongovernmental Indians, Pakistanis, and Americans (with some government officials participating as observers).[27] The group was particularly interested in exploring "whether a new bilateral communications mechanism can reduce the risks of armed conflict and escalation to the nuclear level" (Center for Strategic and International Studies, 2004, p. iv). The group recommended the creation of NRRCs in India and Pakistan to improve communications and reduce the risks for miscalculations leading to nuclear conflict. The group also envisioned that such centers could support the implementation of other related CBMs. According to the final workshop report and discussions with the organizer, the group submitted its findings to both the Indian and Pakistani governments. According to one participant, aspects of the group's work have surfaced in the ongoing India-Pakistan official dialogue process.[28] The group's organizer, Robert Einhorn, believes that "because of the extraordinary

---

[25] Email correspondence with Stimson Center cofounder Michael Krepon, November 15, 2006.

[26] Email correspondence with Michael Krepon, 2006.

[27] For a full list of participants, see Center for Strategic and International Studies (2004, Annexure 1).

[28] Email correspondence with Teresita Schaffer, June 1, 2006.

access to their respective governments enjoyed by our Indian and Pakistani workshop participants, I am sure that our report was conveyed to the highest levels in New Delhi and Islamabad.[29] Indeed, Einhorn deliberately kept the report short and accessible to maximize its policy impact at a particularly opportune time in Indian-Pakistani relations (the group concluded its work several weeks before the resumption of official talks on CBMs).[30]

Cooperative Monitoring Center, Sandia National Laboratories

Since 1994 the CMC at Sandia National Laboratories has hosted training workshops and seminars to foster knowledge about a variety of CBMs that can improve regional security cooperation and lessen tensions in the South Asia (promoting very similar types of programs and exercises as occur in the Middle East arena). Project areas include work on conventional military stability and nuclear risk reduction, nonproliferation and transparency cooperation (with an initial focus on Bangladesh and the monitoring of research reactor operations), and CBMs on less contentious issues such as the environment and water. The programs have produced numerous papers and reports.

Through these workshops, as well as a visiting fellows program, regional participants have developed ideas and collected information that they subsequently brought home to disseminate in academic and official circles. For instance, a former visiting fellow, the current Pakistani ambassador to the United States (Mohammed Durrani) has written widely on cooperative security concepts. Many of the ideas developed at the CMC also influenced official Indian-Pakistani CBMs in recent years.[31] For example, CMC discussions formed the basis of an Indian proposal to establish an organization to monitor the implementation of agreed-upon CBMs that eventually surfaced on the official agenda.[32]

---

[29] Email correspondence with Robert Einhorn, June 9, 2006.

[30] Interview with Robert Einhorn, Washington, D.C., August 28, 2006.

[31] Phone interview with U.S. State Department official, November 14, 2006.

[32] Phone interview with U.S. State Department official, November 14, 2006.

Maritime Activities: The Confidence and Cooperation in South Asian Waters Project

Two research fellows from the Centre for Foreign Policy Studies (CFPS) at Dalhousie University in Canada—Peter Jones and David Griffiths (who were also involved in track two maritime cooperative activities in the Middle East)—began organizing a series of symposia, Confidence and Cooperation in South Asian Waters, in 2001. The first symposium in Lumut, Malaysia, in January 2001 was cohosted by CFPS and the Maritime Institute of Malaysia (MIMA) and cofunded by Canada's Department of Foreign Affairs and International Trade and MIMA. A paper by a Pakistani academic, "Maritime Cooperation between India and Pakistan: Building Confidence at Sea" (Siddiqa-Agha, 2000), formed the basis for the initiative, which brought together former heads of the Indian and Pakistani navies to discuss topics such as prevention of incidents at sea, disputed maritime boundaries, and fishermen imprisoned for straying across the maritime border. The Lumut meeting not only started this dialogue process but also led to the release of almost 600 fishermen.[33]

Subsequent meetings took place in Kuala Lumpur, Malaysia, in April–May 2002 (with financing from the CMC at Sandia National Laboratories and the Canadian government); Delhi, India, in August 2003 at the United Services Institution of India (also financed by the Canadian government); Colombo, Sri Lanka, in August 2003 (again cosponsored by the CMC at Sandia and the Canadian government); Colombo, Sri Lanka, in July 2004 (similar sponsorship as the 2003 symposium); a follow-up meeting to the 2004 workshop for India and Pakistan in New Delhi in July 2005 and Islamabad in August 2005; the fifth annual symposium in Halifax, Nova Scotia, and Washington, D.C., in September 2005 (cohosted by the CFPS and Sandia's CMC). In this last symposium (the project is scheduled to continue), after the retired naval officers met in Halifax to discuss maritime safety and cooperation issues in South Asia waters, the U.S. Department of Energy invited a subgroup to continue discussions on these topics at

---

[33] The details of these meetings and information about the project are published in Dalhousie University Center for Foreign Policy Studies (2006).

the Henry L. Stimson Center and the U.S. Department of State. Seminars on maritime boundaries at these meetings included topics such as jurisdictional zones and entitlements, maritime boundary delimitation, forms of dispute resolution, and transboundary cooperation, including measures that can be pursued without a formal boundary agreement.

Table 3.1 summarizes the track two activities discussed in this chapter.

Roles

Socialization

As in the Middle East, South Asian dialogues have proved rather effective in influencing and shaping the attitudes and ideas of the participating elites. Interviews and surveys with participating elites show that most track two participants find such dialogues useful. One group of analysts who conducted interviews with track two participants found that they "almost universally convey that they have been affected by the experience" (Behera, Evans, and Rizvi, 1997, p. 27). Another survey of South Asian dialogues in the early 1990s found that 42 percent of respondents found such dialogues to be "very useful," while 57.5 percent found them "useful," with no respondents rating such talks as "not useful" (Centre for Policy Research, 1994, pp. 2–3). More critically, this survey found that 77.5 percent of the participants believed the dialogues "succeeded in building a community of South Asian political leaders, scholars and opinion makers," and 75 percent felt that the dialogues "had contributed towards gaining a better understanding of each other's view point" (Centre for Policy Research, 1994, p. 3). As one observer of South Asian arms control dialogues notes, "Academics, bureaucrats, and even military personnel on both sides are in the process of forming an incipient 'epistemic community'" (Ganguly, 1996, p. 14).

One good indicator of socialization is when individuals who participate in track two activities emerge from the process thinking differently, creating pools of like-minded individuals spanning national borders. One Pakistani participant in the Balusa Group, for example,

Table 3.1
Track Two Regional Security Dialogues in South Asia

Track Two Group	Primary Sponsor(s)	Period of Activity	Key Regional Participants' Countries of Origin	Discussion Topics
Neemrana	Ford Foundation, U.S. government	1991–present	India and Pakistan	Regional security, Kashmir, nuclear issues
Balusa	United Nations Development Programmes/ Rockefeller Foundation	1995–present	India and Pakistan	Pakistani-Indian CBMs, Kashmir, economic and energy cooperation (pipeline proposal)
Kashmir Study Group	M. Farooq Kathwari (Kashmiri-American businessman)	1996–present	External participants from the United States, Canada, and Europe; sponsorship of meetings among Pakistanis and Indians	Solution to Kashmir conflict
Shanghai Process	W. Alton Jones, Rockefeller Foundations	1994–2000	India, Pakistan, and China	Proliferation, ballistic missile ban, national security policies
Stimson Center	Private foundations (including Carnegie Corporation, MacArthur Foundation, Nuclear Threat Initiative) and U.S. government	1991–present	India, Pakistan, and China	Regional CBMs and arms control, Kashmir, nuclear risk reduction

Table 3.1 continued

Track Two Group	Primary Sponsor(s)	Period of Activity	Key Regional Participants' Countries of Origin	Discussion Topics
CSIS Nuclear Risk Reduction Project	Nuclear Threat Initiative	2003–2004	India and Pakistan	Nuclear Risk Reduction Centres
Cooperative Monitoring Center, Sandia National Laboratories	U.S. government	2004–present	SAARC members and China	Conventional military stability, nuclear risk reduction, nonproliferation transparency, environmental CBMs
Confidence and Cooperation in South Asian Waters Project	Canadian government, Sandia National Laboratories	2001–2005	India, Pakistan, and Sri Lanka	Maritime CBMs

wrote a book that draws on his experience and discussions from this process, coming to conclusions supportive of cooperative security and CBMs on the political, military, and economic levels (Durrani, 2001). In his book, he reveals that while he "grew up with the firm conviction that the only good Indian was a dead Indian," four years of interaction with Indians in track two dialogues has led him to the conclusion that "Pakistan and India can learn to live in peace with each other" (Durrani, pp. xvii and xix). Such thinking and writing supportive of cooperative security concepts and proposals is now common among many participants who have experienced track two security dialogues in the region, thinking that was largely absent from regional discourse before the 1990s.

Changing mind-sets and perceptions of other regional actors is also a common and often achievable objective for many of these dialogues. Track two venues allow participants to explain national positions and rationales for behavior that are not always transparent in official settings. For example, one American participant noted that Indians often think that the United States is "out to get them" but that unofficial dialogues allow Americans to explain that their policy is based on larger proliferation concerns, not India specifically.[34] South Asian dialogues that include China have also allowed China to better understand Indian positions and the fact that it needs a relationship not just with Pakistan but also with India.[35]

Such discourse also changes what are considered acceptable topics of discussion. For example, the Kashmir Study Group reports that offered novel solutions to the Kashmir conflict were controversial, but they eventually became an acceptable topic of discussion in Pakistan and India.[36] One observer of the Pugwash dialogue on Kashmir noted that such processes facilitate "first hand knowledge of various perspectives on issues like Kashmir" and helped generate a number of CBMs to address problems of the people living on the two sides of the LOC

---

[34] Interview with U.S. State Department official, Washington, D.C., July 1, 2002.

[35] Interview with U.S. State Department official, Washington, D.C., July 1, 2002.

[36] Interview with Teresita Schaffer, Washington, D.C., January 16, 2002, and email correspondence with Schaffer, June 1, 2006.

(Baba 2005). Such dialogues and studies can raise ideas and reframe issues in new ways that can later affect official thinking and form the nucleus of future peace proposals, such as discussions that shift the focus of Kashmir from a territorial dispute between India and Pakistan into a humanitarian issue, focusing on the people living in the region itself.[37] The devastating earthquake in October 2005 that affected both sides of the LOC provided another opportunity to emphasize this alternative perspective.

Track two dialogues have also shaped the thinking of regional elites on the question of nuclear proliferation and arms control, introducing cooperative security concepts and CBMs into the South Asia context. Indeed, the India-Pakistan Neemrana dialogue was sponsored by the U.S. government and explicitly modeled on the U.S.-Soviet Dartmouth Process in an effort to "design and popularize a nuclear restraint regime" (Waslekar, 1995, p. 5). Although the strategic culture of India's elite is realist oriented, some analysts argue that such a mindset does not prevent an openness to arms control and cooperative security concepts, particularly because sectors of India's elite do not view nuclear weapons as morally correct but rather as a risky deterrent.[38]

Moreover, because India's foreign policy and security establishment is increasingly decentralized, some argue that the influence of unofficial thinking, including on critical issues such as nuclear doctrine, is growing: "Non-official thinking has a significant bearing on Indian strategic culture because nuclear weapons in an operational sense are little understood within Indian officialdom, and because the Indian state is in the process of becoming decentralized and more open to non-official inputs."[39] Other South Asia analysts have similarly observed the growing importance of nonstate forces—the media, think tanks, public opinion—in India in influencing the debate on core security issues, including India's nuclear posture:

---

[37] For such a reformulation, see Baba (2005).

[38] See Basur (2001). Basur's analysis explicitly critiques Latham's characterization of Indian strategic culture as realist.

[39] Basur (2001, p. 185). For a comprehensive analysis of India's nuclear posture, see Tellis (2001).

While much of the rationale for India's nuclear policy is technical and scientific. . . . Even analysts without scientific backgrounds are able to comment on such issues due to the information technology revolution that has occurred. . . . Public polls and independent think-tanks are pushing for change (Kasturi, 1999, p. 127).

Track two dialogues also attempt to influence other actors in the security and defense establishments, such as naval officers through military-to-military maritime dialogues. Track two dialogues involving maritime confidence-building proved less contentious than other regional issues and appear to be a productive area for cooperative security practices in both the Middle East and South Asia. There are security analysts who have made the general case that maritime CBMs are a better place to begin conflict resolution among adversaries because of their less contentious nature and clearly mutually beneficial effects (see, for example, Junnola, 1996).

Because conflicts between India and Pakistan have been dominated by the countries' armies and air forces, naval tensions between the adversaries have been more limited, making maritime cooperation in such areas as SAR, INCSEA, and the establishment of a regional maritime risk reduction center "the least volatile of the three dimensions of South Asia war fighting, and thus [offer] the greatest prospects for building upon previous trust that may not be present in other arenas" (Pendharkar, 2003, p. 3). As in the Middle East case, numerous track two dialogues have focused on bringing naval officers together in a range of cooperative maritime activities in unofficial dialogues, leading to large groups of naval officers who have similar training and perspectives and who would like to see elements of their cooperative work elevated to the official level through formal navy-to-navy contacts.[40]

Filtering

As in the case of the Middle East, it is far easier to demonstrate track two dialogues' effect on the participants than to show that such dia-

---

[40] On the need to build on track two naval dialogues to establish track one engagement, see Pendharkar (2003, p. 8).

logues have actually filtered into the thinking and actions of larger segments of society outside of the process itself. That said, the impact of track two in South Asia seems to have gone further than in the Middle East. The growing influence of unofficial actors and public opinion through emerging media outlets, particularly in India, has facilitated the potential for track two dialogue to have greater influence outside the limited group of participating elites.

As noted previously, such unofficial influence is already notable on the nuclear issue in India, particularly as NGOs focused on this issue have grown since the 1998 tests. The ability of nonofficial actors to exert influence on national security issues in Pakistan is more difficult given the military's dominance in national security decisionmaking and virtual veto power on core security issues (arms acquisition, defense expenditure, Kashmir, and the nuclear issue).[41] Still, even in Pakistan, the influence of groups outside the military and formal government institutions, such as intellectuals and journalists, is growing and can allow more track two ideas to filter out of such processes (Mattoo, 1999, p. 308).

Moreover, the involvement of military representatives in track two dialogues can have a direct influence on military thinking and ultimately policy, particularly if such ideas filter to high-level decisionmakers. For instance, the India-Pakistan Neemrana process produced a number of joint research papers by former military officials, including one paper on options for Kashmir that was presented to the Indian and Pakistani governments (Behera, 2002, p. 217). An observer of CMC's work in South Asia believes that the discussions and ideas discussed at Sandia filtered into official thinking, leading in some cases to regional officials' repackaging CMC ideas into their own proposals, such as the Indian initiative to create an organization to monitor the implementation of Indian-Pakistani CBMs.[42]

Another indicator of filtering from track two dialogues is the emergence of regional policy centers focused on issues that are being discussed in track two venues, such as cooperative regional security,

---

[41] Mattoo (1999, p. 311).

[42] Phone interview with U.S. State Department official, November 14, 2006.

regional economic cooperation, Kashmir, and nuclear cooperation. Although many of these research institutes are located in New Delhi, and some even have links to the Indian government, they still are regionally focused and largely independent. An excellent example of a genuinely regional center is the Regional Centre for Strategic Studies (RCSS), based in Colombo, Sri Lanka. The RCSS began in 1992 with the purpose of linking South Asian research institutes and scholars focusing on regional strategic and security issues. Issues of focus and activity have included conceptions of national security, weapon proliferation, CBMs, and broader conflict resolution (see Behera, Evans, and Rizvi, 1997, p. 56). The RCSS also publishes a newsletter and books on regional security topics to disseminate such knowledge to wider regional audiences. Similarly, the RCSS has educated journalists about the nature of CBMs, working on the assumption that if such ideas spread in the media they could ultimately influence governmental thinking.[43] The RCSS also regularly hosts a summer school on defense, technology, and cooperative security in South Asia to target a younger generation of security analysts, as well as a winter workshop on nonmilitary sources of conflict in South Asia (Behera, 2002, p. 220).

Other examples of regionally oriented institutes include the Institute of Peace and Conflict Studie in New Delhi (founded in 1996), the International Center for Peace Initiatives in Mumbai (1990), the Center for Policy Research in New Delhi, the Coalition for Action on South Asian Cooperation in New Delhi (1994), the South Asia Center for Policy Studies (1999), and the South Asia Network of Economic Research Institutes (1998).[44] Such institutes and networks foster a sense of regional ownership and identity by sponsoring regional projects, connecting scholars from across the region, and serving as information clearing houses.[45]

---

[43] Interview with U.S. State Department official, Washington, D.C., July 1, 2002.

[44] For an extensive list of conflict resolution–oriented institutes focused on South Asian security within and outside the region, see Mekenkamp, Tongeren, and van de Veen (2002, pp. 505–618).

[45] For a more detailed review of such institutions, see Waslekar (1995).

Such regional centers are thus providing legitimacy to track two venues and helping to localize such processes. As one South Asia track two observer and participant has noted, "It has become prestigious to be involved in regional conflict resolution efforts. This is a great psychological change since the mid-1980s when conflict resolution used to be dismissed as an irrelevant Western concept" (Waslekar, 1995, p. 8).

The growth of indigenous institutions, centers, and dialogues has also led to a greater number of groups involved in track two discussions. South Asia analysts observe that the "dialogue process has, over the years, broadened its base in terms of participation," with many efforts including previously excluded societal groups, such as women, youth, and parliamentarians (Behera, 2002, p. 229). A regional summer school on arms control and reconciliation targeting young regional strategists, journalists, officials, and scholars has proven particularly successful at broadening and legitimizing regional support for track two activities.[46]

Other dialogues and training seminars similarly focus on the younger generation (the "Midnight's Grandchildren," post-1971 urban middle class youth who are "more cosmopolitan and liberal in outlook") as well as regional parliamentarians and journalists, including indigenous- and regional-language media (Behera, 2002, p. 230). An International Peace Academy project, "Kashmir: New Voices, New Approaches," similarly sought to engage the younger generation of regional scholars to engage and work collaboratively on this challenge.

Policy Impact

As is common in other regionally focused track two security dialogues, the impact of such processes on short-term policy outcomes is minimal. Rarely does such discussion lead to grand policy shifts or radical changes in military postures, nor do participants generally expect such results. One survey of track two participants revealed that only 17.5 percent of respondents believed that such dialogues were effective in influencing government policy (Centre for Policy Research, 1994,

---

[46] Two well-known Western South Asia scholars, George Perkovich and Stephen Cohen, started the summer school in the early 1990s. See Waslekar (1995).

p. 4). Indeed, official policymakers often regard rack two security dialogues with ignorance, suspicion, or hostility, limiting the effect such processes can have on official security policy. Moreover, because South Asia has no formal mechanism for reporting track two activities to government officials, and because participants may be retired officials with limited current government contacts (though there have been important exceptions in which participants have had direct access to official policymakers or later served in official positions themselves), it is difficult for the concepts and proposals of such dialogues to affect official thinking and action. And because track two dialogue is, by its nature, a long-term and incremental process, any effect on official policy may be difficult to detect.

Even so, some impact on official policy is apparent. Some South Asia analysts believe that the political systems in the region—particularly in India—may be developing in ways more conducive to track two influence, particularly on complex issues such as nuclear arms control. For example, one analyst argues, "Non-official thinking has a significant bearing on Indian strategic culture because nuclear weapons in an operational sense are little understood within Indian officialdom" (Basur, 2001, p. 185). Indeed, the Delhi Policy Group—a track two dialogue focused on nuclear reduction and the concept of minimum nuclear deterrence—regularly briefed the foreign offices in both India and Pakistan about its activities (Behera, 2002, p. 213). Given that nonofficial thinking tends to favor nuclear restraint (i.e., keeping the number of deployed nuclear weapons low, avoiding arms racing with China, and favoring arms control and negotiated solutions), an increased influence of this community through track two channels can over time significantly influence official South Asian security policy.

According to another prominent South Asia analyst, ideas based on workshops chaired by Robert Einhorn of CSIS on nuclear risk reduction measures have now surfaced as part of the India-Pakistan official dialogue.[47] Robert Einhorn believes that because the group's report was delivered several weeks before Indian and Pakistani officials began their talks on CBMs in the early summer of 2004, the report was "not

---

[47] Email correspondence with Teresita Schaffer, June 1, 2006.

just delivered; it was read."[48] Indeed, Einhorn asserts that within five days of the completion of the report, it was on President Musharraf's desk and also reached high-level civilian and military Indian officials.[49] Einhorn suggests that "there is evidence that [the report] has had a positive impact on official thinking as those talks have progressed."[50] Similarly, a number of CBMs advocated and nurtured through the Stimson Center dialogues have reached official levels, with several of them ultimately implemented (including the ballistic missile flight test notification agreement, military exercise notifications and constraint measures, and Kashmir-related CBMs). Much of Sandia's CMC work also has influenced official Indian-Pakistani CBMs in recent years.

South Asia has produced other examples of track two influences on policy outside the nonproliferation realm. For instance, the Balusa Group's idea for a joint Indian-Pakistani pipeline to pump natural gas from Iran moved to the official level. As General Durrani (a key member of this group) noted, "Now that the pipeline project seems within grasp, the members of the Balusa Group feel redeemed. What we had thought of as close to a dream is now close to reality" (Hasan, 2006). Given that one of Balusa's founders, Shirin Tahir-Kheli, served as a senior advisor at the U.S. State Department, her experience from Balusa meetings may have significant effects on U.S. foreign policy in this region.

Another example of track two policy impact is a proposal for a Kashmir bus link, initially discussed in the spring of 2000 by Ambassador McDonald of the Institute for Multi-Track Diplomacy, that was formally approved in February 2005 by the foreign ministers of Pakistan and India.[51] Similarly, a high-profile instance of a track two process influencing a track one outcome occurred when the India-Bangladesh dialogues facilitated the resolution of the Farakka Barrage

---

[48] Email correspondence with Robert Einhorn, June 9, 2006.

[49] Interview with Robert Einhorn, Washington, D.C., August 28, 2006.

[50] Email correspondence with Robert Einhorn, June 9, 2006.

[51] The Institute for Multi-Track Diplomacy supports a number of nonofficial dialogues in conflict regions. See its Web site. As of June 18, 2007:
http://www.imtd.org/

dispute between India and Bangladesh and led to the signing of the Ganges Water Treaty (Behera, 2002, p. 214). As one observer of this agreement notes,

> There was an unusual and unprecedented movement of the Track Two participants to the first track of the official dialogues. For instance, from the Indian side, I. K. Gujral, who participated in the dialogue series, subsequently became foreign minister and then the prime minister of India. S. A. M. S. Kibria from Bangladesh was part of the Dhaka delegation to the first two rounds of the dialogue in Delhi and Dhaka on economic relations, and then became the finance minister of Bangladesh (Behera, 2002, p. 214).

However, a negotiator of the Ganges treaty and a foreign secretary of India, Salman Haider, while acknowledging the role of track two groups in getting "thinking going on the subject" and showing that "the problem was soluble," believes that once official negotiations began the solutions of track two groups "did not apply" (quoted in Behera, 2002, p. 214).

Like any policy outcome, it is difficult to demonstrate that only one factor led to the result, and thus it will always be difficult to determine track two's effect, though the existence of its influence, even if limited, is not in doubt. To understand better why this influence is not always as apparent as its promoters and participants might like, the following section considers a number of limitations facing South Asia dialogues.

Limits

Elites

One major limitation of track two's ability to influence and shape official policy in South Asia is the nature of the participating elites. Some elites involved in track two dialogues are still attached to national positions and resist change, making it difficult to reach new understandings on ways to think and act on regional challenges. Such track two participants are often too close to government circles, leading to "status quo" thinking and a continuing divide between those inside and outside the establishment (Behera, 2002, especially p. 227). Because of long-standing nationalistic attitudes, it is difficult to find individuals who are willing and able to think more broadly about a range of regional issues.[52]

That said, while it is difficult to completely screen out ideological hard-liners from track two participation, the majority of participants are usually amenable to forging contacts and hearing new perspectives, as there is a good deal of self-selection involved in dialogue processes (true hard-liners would find little reason to sit at the table with the adversary). But this creates an additional problem related to participation, in that more open-minded elites may not always be the most influential elites and they may have difficulty penetrating well-established thinking in official government circles.

Indeed, in South Asia there is a continued disconnect between track two dialogues and formal government channels. Because decisionmaking on security issues involves small groups of elites in South Asian societies (as is the case in the Middle East), if ideas do not reach these individuals, it becomes difficult to influence policy. As one observer noted, "These ten to twenty people [security elites] do not come to the meetings."[53] Moreover, government officials are often hostile or suspicious of such processes. Official decisionmaking structures in South Asia thus do not encourage track two efforts, nor are there established mechanisms for transferring the track two ideas to officials in positions of power beyond informal and ad hoc contacts. As one observer notes, "With the exception of Bangladesh, bureaucracies have not been pressured from above or below into accepting Track Two or other dialogue processes as a routine part of business, and tend to see few advantages in doing so" (Behera, 2002, p. 226).

Unlike other track two contexts in which there is a high degree of movement of elites from unofficial think tanks and academic institutions into official decisionmaking positions (as in the Asia Pacific),

---

[52] Interview with U.S. State Department official, Washington, D.C., July 1, 2002.

[53] Interview with U.S. State Department official, Washington, D.C., July 1, 2002.

South Asian foreign policy establishments are more insulated and less open to influence from nonofficial channels, although some analysts believe this may be changing with the rise of larger numbers of non-governmental security institutions. Still, in India, for example,

> The foreign-policy bureaucracy, since the Nehru days, has traditionally been the only institution groomed in the task of foreign policymaking. This along with the institutional hurdle of the absence of lateral entry into key bureaucratic positions has resulted in often thick and impermeable barriers . . . an "iron curtain" dividing those "inside" the establishment and those "outside." . . . This is true for every country in South Asia.[54]

Not only is there a barrier between official and unofficial thinking, but many officials who are aware of track two activity have "expressed a disinterest bordering on contempt for involvement of outsiders described in one discussion as 'naïve meddlers and amateurs' lacking the skills and information to manage sensitive issues" (Behera, 2002, pp. 227–228).

Domestic Constraints

The continued mistrust of the adversary among the general public and key domestic institutions within South Asian nations, particularly the military, makes ideas supported by track two—such as cooperative security—difficult to sell to larger constituencies. Skepticism toward regional cooperation is apparent not just in countries where the military is dominant, as in Pakistan, but also among security institutions in democratic India. Indeed, India has traditionally preferred to deal with its neighbors bilaterally (as its dominance is assured) rather than multilaterally, making Indian support for regional multilateral security cooperation difficult. Moreover, some observers of India's strategic culture suggest that India does not believe in balance of power or deterrence, favoring instead a unilateralist and maximalist military posture and global disarmament over regional arms control or nonproliferation (Latham, 1998).

---

[54] Behera (2002, p. 227). For similar ideas, also see Behera (2003).

Because India has not had to face a regional adversary of equal military power, there has been little pressure—at least in strategic terms—for India to shift its security posture toward more cooperative positions (Latham, 1998). India is also extremely suspicious of intervention from outside powers (the U.S. intervention in the 1971 Indian-Pakistani war is a notable example) and thus highly skeptical and cautious about Western efforts to promote regional arms control in track two dialogues.[55] This may help account for why South Asian participants are sensitive to the fact that most funding for such dialogues comes from outside the region, creating "perceptions of external interference," even if participants are genuinely committed to the dialogue process (Behera, 2002, p. 225).

The prevailing strategic mind-set fosters zero-sum thinking and creates an aversion to CBMs, with many Indian participants believing that such initiatives are foreign imports and only benefit adversaries such as Pakistan (Latham, 1998). Indeed, there is regionwide suspicion of CBMs as a "foreign import," and some analysts argue that without less adversarial regional politics it will be difficult for CBMs and other cooperative activity to succeed (Krepon, 1996, p. 7).

Domestic institutions in both India and Pakistan, particularly their intelligence services, are also likely to be hostile to CBMs that would require more transparency in military budgets and defense doctrines.[56] Until foreign and security policy institutions within India, particularly the military, view cooperative security as a benefit rather than a costly imposition, it will be difficult for track two forums to effect progress. The same applies to domestic institutions across the region, although a

---

[55] This point regarding India's resistance to outside intervention was made in an interview with a U.S. State Department official, Washington, D.C., July 1, 2002. Because India is fearful of outside participation, track two dialogues seeking Indian attendance need to include a broad agenda that extends beyond the India-Pakistan relationship to larger questions of nonproliferation that include China. Pakistan, on the other hand, prefers outside intervention and a narrow agenda focused on Kashmir. That said, the Pakistani security establishment is similarly cautious and suspicious when it comes to discussion of cooperative security concepts.

[56] On this point and other barriers to security cooperation in the region, see Ganguly (1996).

positive signal toward track two cooperative security concepts from the region's most powerful nation would send a strong message and could potentially lead to the transformation of regional thinking and policy. However, such shifts have not yet occurred despite the active efforts of regional dialogues to alter these long-standing strategic perspectives.

Regional Environment

In part due to its colonial history and economic links to Europe, South Asia has traditionally had very little intraregional political and economic interaction (see Rizvi, 1993, pp. 147–162), creating a difficult environment for track two efforts seeking to promote greater cooperation, including on contentious security issues. The asymmetric relationship between India and its neighbors and the regional conflicts along India's borders, particularly the ongoing dispute with Pakistan over control of Kashmir, also contribute to a violent regional environment that is not conducive to regional cooperation. Nor is there a commonly perceived external threat propelling South Asians toward greater cooperation as occurred in Europe or Southeast Asia; indeed, security threats are perceived to come primarily from other actors within the region (see Rizvi, 1993, p. 153).

This generally adverse environment for regional cooperation only worsens during violent episodes that impede the progress of track two efforts. For example, the Kargil crisis in 1999 affected the work of several track two activities, making it difficult for some dialogues to sustain organized group sessions between Indians and Pakistanis and leading to more "nationalistic" positions within those groups that did continue to meet (Behera, 2002, p. 229). The continued atmosphere of mistrust and the political vulnerability of the region's leaderships make it difficult to pursue cooperative policies that opposition parties can exploit. This tense regional environment also creates specific logistical problems for dialogues, such as poor airline connections and visa problems for participants.

Conclusion

Despite the inherent limitations of the track two process and its specific constraints in the South Asian context, such dialogues have made significant progress in shaping regional discourse and identity. Not only have track two dialogues socialized a large number of civilian and military elites into thinking about cooperative security and the benefits of working as a region to address common challenges, they have also gone further than has been the case in the Middle East in filtering such ideas to larger segments of society. This is particularly the case as such dialogues expand to new societal groups and lead to the creation of new regional centers, institutes, and advocacy groups.

However, given that the influence of such discourse is long-term and requires a conducive political environment, it is unlikely to lead to immediate and dramatic security policy shifts. Still, examples of track two ideas influencing and leading to concrete official policy proposals are apparent, from notions of a joint India-Pakistan gas pipeline from Iran to initiatives to create NRRCs in the subregion. Moreover, in a favorable regional environment, particularly one in which notable progress is being made in the Indian-Pakistani peace process, it is possible for such dialogues to consolidate the trend toward establishing a regional community and knowledge base supportive of regional cooperation.

CHAPTER FOUR

Conclusion

Central Arguments

Even in conflict-ridden regions such as the Middle East and South Asia, long-standing security postures and military doctrines are not immune to influence and change, particularly as the barriers between official and unofficial societal groups begin to erode. Track two dialogues among influential policy elites focusing on security-related issues are an increasingly important part of the changing landscape in both regions.

While such dialogues rarely lead to dramatic policy shifts and resolution of long-standing regional conflicts, they have played a significant role in shaping the views, attitudes, and knowledge bases of core groups of security elites, both civilian and military, and in some instances have begun to filter the ideas discussed into wider segments of society. In South Asia, some track two initiatives have directly influenced the content of official Indian-Pakistani CBMs on Kashmir and nonproliferation. But any notable influence on policy from such efforts is likely to be long-term, due to the nature of the activity and the many limitations and constraints of carrying out such discussions in regions vastly different from the West.

Thus, track two dialogues on regional security are not as much about producing high-profile official diplomatic breakthroughs as they are about socializing an influential group of security elites to think in more cooperative ways. They are less about humanizing the enemy—as important as this may be—than about demonstrating that security cooperation with an adversary (or indeed even with friendly regional neighbors) can reinforce, rather than undermine, national security interests. Track two dialogues can alter views about the value of cooperation with other regional actors, even if attitudes toward those actors remain generally negative. Such dialogues are thus best viewed as social processes whereby problems and their responses can be defined by influential groups, leading to the *potential* for greater regional cooperation and perhaps other related policy shifts over time (e.g., formal arms control measures, altered military doctrines, and nonaggression pacts).

Indeed, encouraging actors to recalculate the value of cooperation with one's neighbors and consider cooperative security concepts and postures has proven among the most valuable roles for track two dialogues in regions such as the Middle East and South Asia. A narrow focus on policy change would miss the crux of what track two dialogues are about—changing the regional psychology regarding long-standing security positions and creating a vast network of influential policy elites who are more receptive to ideas supportive of cooperative security and dialogue. Such dialogues also underscore the complexity of regional challenges and move regional thinking away from the idea that regional stability depends solely on the resolution of one political conflict. Track two is an attempt to reshape the strategic mind-set and culture in nations and regions with long histories of violent conflict, to work toward less-competitive security postures and approach regional security issues in novel ways.

Such reframing of security perceptions and postures can be successful only when regional elites view such change as in their own interests, and not as a favor to external Western supporters or a condition of strong relations with the West. Making track two dialogues and the ideas promoted by them an indigenous process is thus crucial for their success. Without such adaptation to local environments, track two supporters who attempt to sell and spread track two ideas to their own governments and societies will never be viewed as legitimate, nor will there be a real reconceptualization of interests beyond tactical adjustments to address Western concerns.

Despite these challenges, the ability of relatively small groups of influential policy networks to shift national and regional discourse should not be underestimated. Networks of anti-Western extremist groups have crossed national boundaries in recent years and have reached wider audiences in part through the information revolution, particularly the growth of satellite television, the Web, and new media outlets independent of government control (Lynch, 2006). There is no reason why moderate regional voices arguing for reconciliation and cooperation—based on self-interest rationales—could not also utilize such outlets to influence national and regional debates.

The beginning of the 21st century is proving a volatile time for the Middle East and South Asia. Change can be for the better or worse, depending on which regional ideas prevail. Track two dialogues involve largely moderate voices that have the potential to influence the future in a more positive direction, and the stakes are high. Greater understanding of track two dialogues should lead to less skepticism and indifference toward such activities and a more concerted investment and careful promotion of these dialogues both inside and outside the regions.

Regional Comparisons

Chapters Two and Three underscore the ways in which the Middle East and South Asia face similarly hostile environments for cooperative security concepts promoted through track two dialogues. Neither in the Middle East nor in South Asia is there a common perception of external or internal threats that might propel the regional actors toward greater regional cooperation; instead, threat perceptions are more often based on actors from within the region or even from within respective societies (Rizvi, 1993, p. 153).

One could argue that the rising power of Iran may serve as a regional unifier in the Middle East in the years to come, but such an external threat is unlikely to overcome the animosity between Arabs and Israelis (or among Arabs themselves) and generate the political will needed for sustained regional cooperation. Moreover, large Shi'a populations within Arab states and Iranian links to significant nongovernmental groups (such as Hezbollah and Hamas) capable of fomenting instability could lead to cautionary policies with respect to Iran and perhaps more accommodation, or at least hedging, than confrontation. Furthermore, the tendency of regional actors to align bilaterally with external powers as insurance against regional threats, rather than create multilateral cooperative security arrangements, will be difficult to overcome.[1]

Such environments contrast with the European experience, in which the external threat of the Soviet Union (as well as the economic challenge of both the United States and Japan) and the internal threat perception of communist subversion served as a unifying force. Southeast Asia also relied on common perceptions of external threats (Soviet and Chinese influence in the region) and the internal threat of communism to solidify mechanisms and institutions for regional cooperation (see Rizvi, 1993, p. 153). Active U.S. support for creating a multilateral security structure in Europe also contributed to a culture supportive of regional cooperation. In contrast, U.S. support—diplomatic or financial—for regional security groupings in regions such as the Middle East and South Asia is either lacking, ambivalent, or passive, despite the greater U.S. military presence in both regions and a growing U.S. role in conflict mediation.

Both the Middle East and South Asia are also dominated by security elites with realist mind-sets in which competitive and zero-sum thinking are pervasive, making track two ideas supportive of cooperative security a tough sell. Cooperative security is also a difficult concept in regions where the conventional wisdom is that nuclear weapons are vital for security and where the risks associated with such weapons are not widely understood or acknowledged. Moreover, the most powerful actors in both regions—Israel and India—do not view arms control as a vital national interest, nor are they inclined to support regional multilateral security forums, preferring instead bilateral security arrangements with regional neighbors and external actors.

Both India and Israel also have a similar approach to the sequencing of cooperative security and the arms control process, with each pre-

---

[1] On the possibilities of new regional security architectures in the Middle East in the aftermath of the Iraq war, see Kaye (unpublished RAND research).

ferring to first pursue broad agendas of CBMs that address a range of regional issues before focusing on the core issues that their adversaries seek to highlight (nuclear weapons and the Palestinian track in the case of Israel, and Kashmir in the case of India).[2] Indeed, to the extent that cooperative security forums have emerged in the two regions, external Western actors have largely promoted them.

Another similarity apparent in both the Middle East and South Asia is that confidence-building and track two dialogues cannot replace political processes. Resolution of the core political disputes in each region (Palestine and Kashmir) is ultimately a necessary condition for reconciliation and stability, though certainly not a sufficient one. The purpose of track two dialogues in both regions is to help change fundamental political relationships by changing the thinking on both sides, but the influence of such dialogues also depends on the state of the political environment at any given time. In this way, the official and nonofficial processes are mutually dependent.

Both regions also face similar regional economic dynamics, making regional cooperation more difficult. Underdevelopment and low intraregional trade (South Asia's intraregional trade is less than 5 percent of its total world trade; in the Middle East it is approximately 7 percent of the total) pose significant barriers to cooperative economic schemes. This suggests that greater economic cooperation would lead to a more conducive environment for security cooperation. As one South Asia scholar supportive of a cooperative security paradigm explains, "Promoting greater regional economic and political cooperation could definitely ameliorate national security problems in the region" (Chari, 1999, p. 419). In the context of globalization debates in the 1990s, many Middle East and South Asian elites also raised the "guns versus butter" debate, arguing that cooperative security paradigms might help address and alleviate economic conditions in developing nations.[3] But

---

[2] On India's approach, see Chari (1999, pp. 457–458). On Israel's approach to regional security and arms control, see Jentleson and Kaye (1998).

[3] Former Israeli prime minister and foreign minister Shimon Peres, for example, was a high-profile proponent of the need to refocus regional energy into development rather than continued military spending and arms racing (Peres, 1993). Durrani (2001) also supports such logic in the South Asia context.

such ideas failed to lead to significant policy change and did not capture the imagination of wide audiences in either region. Traditional security mind-sets continue to prevail well into the 21st century.

Because of these challenging regional environments and difficulties in changing mind-sets at the official level, regional elites in both the Middle East and South Asia turned to track two dialogues to pursue cooperative security agendas. They were inspired to do so largely because of the changing international security and economic environment following the Cold War, as well as greater appreciation of the role civil society can play in reducing regional tensions.[4] The 1998 nuclear tests in India and Pakistan also facilitated interest and dialogue on nuclear stability regimes, drawing on lessons from the East-West experience for South Asia and leading to new groups of regional analysts and activists devoted to crafting a more stable nuclear relationship on the subcontinent.

Indeed, the socialization aspect of track two dialogues has proved rather effective in both cases. Thousands of military and civilian elites have been exposed to cooperative security concepts and activities, creating the beginnings of cross-border constituencies in both regions. Knowledge of complex arms control and regional security concepts and operational confidence-building activity is now solidly rooted among these elites.

That said, track two efforts in both regions faced the dilemma whereby a large group of security elites have begun to think in similar ways, but their influence on official thinking and policy has been limited. Policy impact has fallen short either because such elites are out of the decisionmaking loop or because their spreading of ideas to the official level has been informal, ad hoc, and episodic. In contrast to ASEAN, neither region has institutional mechanisms that support track two activities, and both lack official mentors who can advocate the ideas emerging from such processes. The fact that most track two dialogues are still funded from outside, largely Western sources also has challenged the legitimacy of such efforts and limited their effectiveness.

---

[4]   On this point of the changing role of civil society in conflict resolution, see Yaffe (2001).

Despite such similarities—leading to largely negative expectations for track two's effect in both regions—some significant differences are also apparent, suggesting slightly more positive assessments in the case of South Asia. For instance, the public in South Asia is generally more supportive of reconciliation than in the Middle East, particularly because, in South Asia, recognition of key regional actors and diplomatic relations is the norm, unlike the situation in the Middle East, in which normalization with Israel is still taboo among many governments and the majority of people in the region.[5] This fundamental difference, along with factors such as the existence of a regional institution in South Asia (SAARC)—even if weak—and the previous record of Indian and Pakistani negotiations on formal CBMs (such as agreements not to attack the other's nuclear facilities, advance warning for troop maneuvers, and direct communication between the directors-general of military operations), have led some analysts to conclude that cooperative security and confidence-building may be easier in South Asia than in the Middle East (Heller, 1996, p. 116).

India and Pakistan (and others in the region, including Bangladesh and Nepal) are also culturally similar despite poor political relations. Cultural affinities (e.g., food, music, television, dress) are rich and numerous, creating greater potential for peace constituencies to develop at the grassroots level. The popularity of new bus links in Kashmir between the Indian and Pakistani sides of the LOC seems to support such logic. The opening of the LOC following the devastating earthquake in the region in October 2005 may continue to facilitate the expansion of people-to-people contacts and ease political tensions in the face of humanitarian crisis.

In the Arab-Israeli context, there are far fewer cultural and political connections. (Of course, inter-Arab dialogues do not face this problem, although the inclusion of Iran in Gulf dialogues would create significant cultural gaps and highlight sensitivities related to Sunni-Shi'a divisions, particularly in the aftermath of the sectarian bloodlet-

---

[5]   On the difference between the Middle East and other regional experiences in confidence-building due to the legitimacy and recognition problem leading to the existential nature of the Arab-Israeli conflict, see Heller (1996).

ting in Iraq.) Arabs who support reconciliation with Israel are still out on a limb and risk public exposure that could cost them their jobs or even their physical safety. Most societal groups in the Arab world still oppose normalization with Israel.[6] In the Middle East, Arab governments are ahead of the public in terms of reconciliation with Israel; in South Asia, the reverse appears to be the case.

Perhaps because South Asia's public is more receptive of reconciliation efforts, track two ideas are spreading to more societal groups in South Asia and leading to the development of more cooperative regional centers. These developments could also be linked to the stronger tradition of democracy in South Asia, as the rapid growth of regional cooperation centers and institutes in India seems to suggest. Open discussion of the nuclear issue in South Asia since the 1998 tests has also increased as advocacy groups focusing on the issue have developed. Nuclear activism is still unheard of in the Middle East.

Consequently, South Asia seems to carry more filtering potential for unofficial dialogues than the Middle East at present. More democratic openings in the Middle East or a nuclear arms race sparked by Iran could change the equation and encourage widespread questioning among societal groups regarding key tenets of national security policy. But such change in the Middle East could also worsen the prospects for more cooperative postures and political reconciliation, since many nongovernmental groups in the region are not supportive of peace with Israel, taking more hard-line positions on peace process issues than their governments. And the pursuit of nuclear programs may be popular among populations concerned about restoring the status and influence of regional states after many decades of external meddling.

---

[6] After the 1991 Gulf War and particularly the Oslo peace talks in 1993, much debate emerged in the Arab world regarding normalization with Israel, and some new ties began to emerge among Israel, North African states (such as Morocco), and small Gulf states, even leading to small Israeli missions in cities such as Rabat. However, public opinion remained opposed to such normalization efforts, and after the demise of the peace process, beginning with Yitzhak Rabin's assassination in October 1995, normalization efforts froze. For a review of such developments in the 1990s, see Kaye (2001a). More recently, since the Israeli unilateral withdrawal and the death of Yassir Arafat, which has led to some resumption of Israeli-Palestinian negotiations, normalization debates are again emerging. See, for example, Fattah (2005).

Regional Lessons

When the Middle East peace process seemed to be advancing dramatically in the early 1990s, following the Israeli-Palestinian Oslo Accords in September 1993, some South Asians began asking why their region's conflict resolution efforts were lagging behind. This led to studies speculating what South Asia might learn from the Middle East experience in peacemaking, particularly from track two channels such as the Oslo process (see, for example, Ahmar, 2001). The surprising progress made by the first official Arab-Israeli regional multilateral security forum following the 1991 Madrid peace talks—the multilateral ACRS Working Group—also suggested some potential for Western-style operational and conceptual CBMs to be applied to other regions in conflict, although the breakdown of the process after only three years of activity also highlighted the limits of such efforts.

But with the deterioration of the Israeli-Palestinian track and the resumption of an Indian-Pakistani peace process in recent years, the tables have turned to some extent. The more appropriate question now might be what the Middle East might learn from South Asia. Although such observations are based on short-term developments and atmospherics in each region at any given time (the prospects for peace fluctuate rapidly in both regions as dramatic openings and progress are often quickly derailed by acts of terrorism or changes of leadership), there are more static realities that suggest that South Asia might be a better model, or at least a predictor, for the Middle East than vice versa.

The most significant of these realities is the fact that South Asia is now an openly nuclear region, a situation unlikely to reverse itself in the near future. This development following the 1998 tests led to widespread concern about the effectiveness of global nonproliferation efforts (although neither India nor Pakistan were signatories of the NPT, creating a new category of nuclear non-NPT states, of which Israel is also a member despite its formal policy of nuclear ambiguity). Many analysts were also concerned that the Indian-Pakistani nuclear relationship would not follow the stability of U.S.-Soviet deterrence models and that the potential for miscalculation and accidents could lead to catastrophic results.[7]

There is particular concern over the safety of Pakistan's nuclear arsenal given the domestic instability in that country and the lack of civilian control of the military, in addition to fears that Pakistan's technology could spread (following the Abdul Qadeer Khan example).[8] The growing disparity in the military balance between India and Pakistan (with India dominating on both a quantitative and qualitative basis) can also be a source of future instability, leading to scenarios that suggest more aggressive Indian behavior (see Peters et al., 2006).

Such concerns are likely to be replicated and viewed with even more alarm if Iran acquires a nuclear weapon capability. This is particularly the case given that nuclear breakout is unlikely to remain a bipolar relationship between Israel and Iran but, rather, is more likely to lead to a multipolar nuclear region.[9] As in the case of South Asia, many analysts worry that the Cold War model of nuclear stability will not hold in such a scenario. Indeed, the multipolar nature of a future nuclear Middle East could prove even more destabilizing than the current situation in South Asia, in which at least the nuclear issue is contained to two central adversaries.

Still, the nuclear restraint regime that has been developing between India and Pakistan (and the fact that this is taking place despite the complicating factor of China's nuclear position and its effect on India) offers concrete examples for future arrangements in the Middle East to

---

[7] On nuclear accident and safety issues, see Sagan (1993). For a pessimistic assessment of nuclear stability in South Asia, see Joeck (1997).

[8] For a discussion of Pakistan's nuclear weapons posture and strategy, see Durrani (2004). General Durrani is not alarmist about the threat of proliferation from Pakistan's arsenal, but he does argue that the Indian-Pakistani deterrence relationship is unstable given the continuation of territorial disputes, mistrust, a lack of institutionalized crisis management mechanisms, and a lack of understanding of nuclear strategy and deterrence (see especially p. 32).

[9] If Iran acquires a nuclear weapon capability, there are plausible cases to be made that Arab states, including Saudi Arabia and Egypt, might attempt to follow, as might other regional actors, such as Turkey. Israel would also be under pressure to reveal its nuclear capabilities for deterrent purposes. On the regional implications of a nuclear Iran, see Kaye and Wehrey (2007), Yaphe and Lutes (2005), and Sokolski and Clawson (2005).

reduce the likelihood of nuclear accidents or escalation. Indeed, some analysts of India's nuclear posture suggest that because a rollback of nuclear capabilities in South Asia is unlikely, the focus should shift to building an effective nuclear restraint regime and bolstering escalation-control mechanisms.[10]

Such restraints have been more apparent than alarmist reactions to a nuclear South Asia might suggest, and imply that nuclear restraint and security cooperation are possible even among bitter adversaries. An analyst of India's nuclear position argues that India's natural disposition is toward moderation: "Left to its own devices, New Delhi will more likely than not pursue strategic programs that are more or less modest in their scope and orientation" (Tellis, 2001, p. 762). Thus, despite continuing dangers and uncertainties, India and Pakistan have already engaged in well-advanced nuclear CBMs that can serve as an important record for Middle Eastern actors looking for guidance if their region becomes nuclear.[11] Ideas focused on creating a nuclear *safe* zone in South Asia[12]—as opposed to a more ambitious nuclear *free* zone—will be an especially important experiment that Middle Easterners will want to closely track.

While the South Asian nuclear experience raises important lessons for the Middle East, the more immediate reality since the 1998 nuclear tests is that nuclear weapons have had more of an impact on conventional rather than unconventional warfare. The potential for nuclear weapon capabilities to lead to greater aggressiveness and conflict on the conventional battlefield has played out in South Asia and offers a cautionary message for future Middle East security relationships.

The logic of such developments follows the stability-instability dilemma, whereby "the 'stability' induced in bilateral adversarial rela-

---

[10] See Tellis (2001). Other analysts also argue that a stable nuclear-deterrence relationship between India and Pakistan is possible and that the West should be actively engaged in promoting such a relationship. See Heisbourg (1998–1999).

[11] For a list of relevant CBMs and communications measures related to the nuclear issue, see Center for Strategic and International Studies (2004, Annexure 2).

[12] On ideas for a nuclear safe zone—including declarations on no first use, no use against non-nuclear powers, and no use against populations—see Mattoo (1999, pp. 326–329).

tions by constructing a nuclear deterrent relationship could be offset by the 'instability' resulting from the feasibility of a conventional war becoming greater."[13] Nuclear capabilities can provide the cover for regional actors to launch conventional campaigns while deterring adversaries from escalating the conflict (see Chari, 2005). In essence, nuclear-deterrence "stability" makes conventional "instability" (with self-imposed constraints) more likely.[14] The development of post-1998 conventional crises—particularly the Kargil conflict in 1999 and the border confrontation between India and Pakistan following a terrorist attack on the Indian parliament in late 2001—seems to support such logic and suggests a dangerous precedent for the Middle East. Although the post-1998 conflicts were ultimately contained, in large part due to the role of the United States,[15] the idea that nuclear weapons may make the potential for armed conventional warfare even higher—in a region already dominated by multiple armed conflicts—is sobering.

As a prominent South Asia nuclear analyst observes:

> Nuclear weapons, in theory, can only deter nuclear weapons and large-scale conventional wars. But, South Asian conflict has

---

[13] Chari, (2003). Chari (2003, footnote 65, p. 19) also cites Charles L. Glaser's formulation of the concept from his book (1990), which states that "lowering the probability that a conventional war will escalate to a nuclear war—along preemptive and other lines—reduces the danger of starting a conventional war; thus, this low likelihood of escalation—referred to here as 'stability'—makes conventional war less dangerous, and possibly, as a result, more likely."

[14] S. Paul Kapur (2005) offers a strong challenge to the causal logic of this thesis, although his analysis suggests a similar outcome: conventional instability. However, in Kapur's view, this is not because of the stability of the nuclear strategic environment but rather because of its instability. In this analysis, the risk of nuclear confrontation is real and is used by Pakistan to provide cover and deter India from launching a full-scale conventional attack on Pakistan. In this sense, the instability of the nuclear relationship in South Asia suggests a significantly different model than the Cold War relationship between the United States and the Soviet Union, and one that is likely to have more relevance to the Middle East.

[15] On the role of the United States in mediating these conflicts, see Chari (2005, especially p. 25). The importance of external factors in contributing to escalation control and conflict mediation, particularly the United States with its military stationed in both regions, is also an important model for future crises likely to develop in the Middle East context if and when the region goes nuclear.

decisively entered subterranean channels like proxy wars, clandestine operations, cross-border terrorism and so on, illustrating the operations of the "stability-instability paradox" in a special geo-political setting. Subterranean conflicts now flourish in South Asia, raising problems for escalation control (Chari, 2005, p. 23).

Given that the Middle East security environment resembles such a geo-political setting, a future multipolar nuclear Middle East will likely be wrestling with similar dilemmas and dangers. The conflict in Lebanon in the summer of 2006 underscored the dangers that a nuclear-armed Iran might pose through its use of regional proxies such as Hezbollah. These dangers underscore the need to utilize track two security dialogues to create and improve channels of communication among regional adversaries and lay the groundwork for conceptual and operational CBMs that will help prevent or at least contain future conflicts, at both the conventional and unconventional levels.

Improving Track Two Dialogues

Expand the Types of Participants

One way to expand track two ideas to larger segments of society is to include broader types of representatives in such processes, on the condition that such participants are still influential, either in government circles or within key constituencies within a nation (or have the potential to be future decisionmakers). One area that is proving effective is bringing younger generations of security analysts into such processes through education programs like the summer school on arms control in South Asia started by Stephen Cohen of the Brookings Institution. Additional training courses for diplomats and defense officials, especially younger ones, about the nature and purpose of track two dialogues can help sensitize officials to the value of such efforts and perhaps create future support for such efforts.

Others suggest that including more politicians, business groups, and journalists in track two dialogues would further build regional support for new political relationships and cooperation, since such groups are better connected to large grassroots constituencies. In this regard, it is especially important to include representatives from all political parties, both ruling and opposition, including groups perceived to be opposed to conflict resolution efforts. Such groups can potentially produce "entrepreneurial leaders" who are more likely to "break out of established patterns and to move forward on a concrete security-building agenda" (Latham, 1998, p. 236). Efforts in South Asia to create unofficial dialogues for parliamentarians could be continued and strengthened,[16] and such processes could be established in the Middle East context as well.

The other critical group whose involvement should be expanded is the military. Educating regional militaries in similar concepts and changing their thinking regarding the value of security cooperation is essential for any future shifts in national security doctrines and policies. Regardless of the nature of civil-military relations in any given country (i.e., whether the country has civilian control over its military or not), military establishments are important players in negotiations over CBMs. As South Asia analysts observe, "Unless the professional military is convinced of the utility of CSBMs, they will not be agreed [to] and implemented" (Ganguly and Greenwood, 1996). Track two dialogues in both regions have shown that military-to-military discussions often break new ground and are more open to new ideas than are discussions dominated by the political elite, as the notable progress in maritime cooperation among regional navies illustrates. Some track two participants have suggested that because military representatives are more attune to the risks of war, they are more capable of developing new ideas when they meet their regional counterparts. This may be especially true in the case of India and Pakistan, whose militaries developed from the British army and thus inherited similar organizational cultures.[17]

Beyond military contacts, expanding track two dialogues to include intelligence analysts might also help foster better under-

---

[16] On such efforts, see Behera (2002, p. 230).

[17] This observation is based on an interview with an American analyst, Washington, D.C., January 16, 2002.

standings of mutual threat perceptions and increase support for more restrained and cooperative policies over time. Those who do participate should be encouraged to disseminate the ideas discussed in track two settings into their local environments to the extent that this is politically possible, such as through editorials, media interviews, or briefings to key senior officials.

Create or Strengthen Institutional Support and Mentors for Track Two Activities

Regional governments could be quietly more supportive of track two activity. For example, one analyst suggests that Indian policymakers could be less cynical about track two forums and could do a better job of finding ways to show that "track-two deliberations are valued and can carry weight with incumbent policy makers," such as by treating track two invitees better and issuing less restrictive visas for attendance at such meetings (Mattoo, 1999, p. 333). In other words, track two dialogues should not just be "tolerated but actively encouraged" (Mattoo, 1999, p. 333). Another observer and participant of track two diplomacy in the Middle East similarly argues,

> Regional governments will need to show imagination. They will have to accept the notion that policy ideas (though not policy itself) can be developed outside strictly official channels. Indeed, they will have to encourage this with financial, human and other resources over time (Jones 2005c).

Regional institutions can also play a role in strengthening and legitimizing track two dialogues. SAARC, despite its limitations, is an important arena for regional elites to meet and discuss bilateral issues on the margins of the meetings.[18] In fact, SAARC could serve as a useful model for the Middle East in future efforts to revive the multilateral peace process that addressed a variety of "functional" regional

---

[18] Some South Asia analysts challenge overly pessimistic assessments of SAARC's achievements and argue that the institution has served as an important mechanism for fostering regional cooperation; its main limitation has been less the nature of the institution than the lack of political will to give it more teeth. See Chari (1999, p. 463).

issues, including regional arms control and security, economic development, the environment, water, and refugees. A future Middle East association for regional cooperation could serve as a focal point for regional cooperative efforts and encourage unofficial thinking on contentious regional issues and bilateral disputes. Such an institution could generate broad regional support by focusing first on less contentious issues, such as humanitarian relief operations.

In Southeast Asia, ASEAN has proved an important institutional mechanism for track two efforts and ideas to filter to the highest levels of policymakers; such types of regional institutions could serve similar purposes in the Middle East and South Asia. Although various institutions in the region address regional security issues, these institutions are not "linked together in a system of ongoing Track Two. . . . This is not just a matter of money. An indigenous community of experts needs to be established" (Jones, 2005c, p. 16). Even if regional institutions may take time to develop, regional centers, such as the RCSS in Colombo, can also help build such communities. These types of centers are needed in the Middle East as well. Such centers can foster networks of individuals and institutions devoted to issues of regional security and cooperation.

Localize the Dialogues

Finally, track two processes are more likely to have an effect if they are perceived as indigenous. Although most track two efforts could not survive without external funding, even symbolic regional contributions to support such dialogues are important and underscore that regionals are participating because such dialogues serve their own interests and are not simply a favor to outside actors. Meetings should also take place in the region, to the extent that the security environment and political considerations allow.

Legitimacy is a very important element for the success of such efforts and their ability to spread the ideas discussed in small groups to wider segments of society. Such legitimacy is not possible if track two dialogues are widely viewed as a Western imposition. Consequently, promoters of track two dialogues need to be aware of such sensitivities and work toward building regional constituencies and institutions supportive of track two dialogues. Following these recommendations will not ensure the success of track two diplomacy in regions such as the Middle East and South Asia, but it can certainly contribute to less hostile and war-prone environments for the people living there.

Bibliography

Abidi, Zawar Haider, *Threat Reduction in South Asia*, Washington, D.C.: Henry L. Stimson Center, November 2003. As of June 18, 2007:
http://www.stimson.org/pub.cfm?id=87

Acharya, Amitav, "Culture, Security, Multilateralism: The 'ASEAN Way' and Regional Order," *Contemporary Security Policy*, Vol. 19, No. 1, April 1998, pp. 55–84.

———, "How Ideas Spread: Whose Norms Matter? Norm Localization and Institutional Change in Asian Regionalism," *International Organization*, Vol. 58, No. 2, Spring 2004a, pp. 239–275.

———, "An Asian Perspective," in Martin Ortega, ed., *Global Views on the European Union*, Chaillot Paper No. 72, Paris: Institute for Security Studies, November 2004b, pp. 93–102.

Adler, Emanuel, "The Emergence of Cooperation: National Epistemic Communities and the International Evolution of the Idea of Nuclear Arms Control," *International Organization*, Vol. 46, No. 1, Winter 1992, pp. 101–145.

Adler, Emanuel, and Michael Barnett, eds., *Security Communities*, Cambridge, UK: Cambridge University Press, 1998.

Afrasiabi, Kaveh L., "Iran Unveils a Persian Gulf Security Plan" *Asia Times*, April 14, 2007. As of June 14, 2007:
http://www.atimes.com/atimes/Middle_East/ID14Ak04.html

Agha, Hussein, Shai Feldman, Ahmad Khalidi, and Zeev Schiff, *Track-II Diplomacy: Lessons from the Middle East*, Cambridge, Mass.: MIT Press, 2003.

Agha, Hussein, and Aharon Levran, *Commmon Ground on Lebanon: A Lebanese-Israeli Dialogue*, Washington, D.C.: Initiative for Peace and Cooperation in the Middle East, 1992.

Ahmar, Moonis, ed., *The Arab-Israeli Peace Process: Lessons for India and Pakistan*, Oxford: Oxford University Press, 2001.

Al-Ahram Center for Political and Strategic Studies, Consortium of Research Institutes' Project on Regional Co-Operation and Security in the Middle East and North Africa, 2004. As of June 14, 2007:
http://www.ahram.org.eg/acpss/eng/ahram/2004/7/5/semi3.htm

Al Attiya, Abdul Rahman, "The Declaration of the Gulf WMDFZ Initiative by the GCC Secretary-General," reprinted in Gulf Research Center (undated). Original sources listed as *Asharq Al Awast*, December 19, 2005, and *Agence France-Presse*, December 18, 2005.

Asmus, Ronald D., "Contain Iran: Admit Israel to NATO," *Washington Post*, February 21, 2006, p. A15.

Asmus, Ronald D., Larry Diamond, Mark Leonard, and Michael McFaul, "A Transatlantic Strategy to Promote Democratic Development in the Broader Middle East," *The Washington Quarterly*, Vol. 28, No. 2, Spring 2005, pp. 7–21.

Baba, Noor Ahmad, "Pugwash Conference on Kashmir: Some Reflections," Institute of Peace and Conflict Studies, Article No. 1620, January 20, 2005. As of June 17, 2007:
http://www.ipcs.org/newKashmirLevel2.jsp?action=
showView&kValue=1633&subCatID=null&mod=null

Baker, James A. III, and Lee H. Hamilton, co-chairs, *The Iraq Study Group Report*, New York: Vintage Books, 2006.

Basur, Rajesh M., "Nuclear Weapons and Indian Strategic Culture," *Journal of Peace Research*, Vol. 38, No. 2, March 2001.

Behera, Navnita Chadha, "Forging New Solidarities: Nonofficial Dialogues," in Monique Mekenkamp, Paul van Tongeren, and Hans van de Veen, eds., *Searching for Peace in Central and South Asia*, Boulder, Colo.: Lynne Rienner Publishers, 2002.

———, "Need to Expand Track-Two Diplomacy," *Asia Times*, July 16, 2003. As of June 25, 2007:
http://www.atimes.com/atimes/South_Asia/EG16Df03.html

Behera, Navnita Chadha, Paul M. Evans, and Gowher Rizvi, *Beyond Boundaries: A Report of the State of Non-Official Dialogues on Peace, Security and Cooperation in South Asia*, North York, Ontario: University of Toronto–York University Joint Centre for Asia Pacific Studies, 1997.

Bhargava, Kant Kishore, Heinz Bongartz, and Farooq Sobhan, eds., *Shaping South Asia's Future: Role of Regional Cooperation*, New Delhi: Vikas Publishing House, 1995.

Burton, John, and Frank Dukes, eds., *Conflict: Readings in Management of Resolution*, New York: St. Martin's Press, 1990.

Buzan, Barry, and Ole Waever, *Regions and Powers: The Structure of International Security*, Cambridge, UK: Cambridge University Press, 2003.

Center for Strategic and International Studies, *Nuclear Risk Reduction Centres in South Asia*, Working Group Report, Washington, D.C., May 2004. As of June 17, 2007:
http://www.csis.org/media/csis/pubs/0406_nrrcreport.pdf

Centre for Policy Research, *South Asian Regional Dialogue 1991–1993: An Assessment*, November 1994.

Chari, P. R., "Towards a New Paradigm for National Security," in P. R. Chari, ed., *Perspectives on National Security in South Asia*, New Delhi: Manohar Publishers, 1999, pp. 457–458.

———, "Nuclear Crisis, Escalation Control, and Deterrence in South Asia," Washington, D.C.: Henry L. Stimson Center, Working Paper, Version 1.0, August 2003.

———, "Limited War Under the Nuclear Shadow in South Asia," Institute of Peace and Conflict Studies, Article No. 1623, January 29, 2005. As of March 4, 2005:
http://www.ipcs.org/Nuclear_seminars2.jsp?action=showView&kValue=1636

Checkel, Jeffrey T., "The Constructivist Turn in International Relations Theory," *World Politics*, Vol. 50, No. 2, January 1998, pp. 324–348.

———, "Building New Identities? Debating Fundamental Rights in European Institutions," ARENA Working Paper, 2000. As of June 18, 2007:
http://www.arena.uio.no/publications/wp00_12.htm

———, "Why Comply? Social Learning and European Identity Change," *International Organization*, Vol. 55, No. 3, August 2001, pp. 553–588.

Cook, Steven A., *The Unspoken Power: Civil-Military Relations and the Prospects for Reform*, Washington, D.C.: Brookings Institution, 2004.

Cooperative Monitoring Center–Amman, homepage, undated. As of July 18, 2007:
http://www.cmc-amman.gov.jo/

Council for Security Cooperation in the Asia Pacific, homepage, last updated January 4, 2006. As of June 13, 2007:
http://www.cscap.org/

Crawford, Neta, *Argument and Change in World Politics: Ethics, Decolonization, and Humanitarian Intervention*, Cambridge, UK: Cambridge University Press, 2002.

Dalhousie University Centre for Foreign Policy Studies, homepage, last updated June 17, 2007. As of July 18, 2007:
http://centreforforeignpolicystudies.dal.ca/index.php

————, "Confidence and Cooperation in South Asian Waters," July 21, 2006. As of June 17, 2007:
http://centreforforeignpolicystudies.dal.ca/events/marsec_CCSAW.php

Davidson, W. D., and J. V. Montville, "Foreign Policy According to Freud," *Foreign Policy*, Vol. 45, Winter 1981–1982.

Davies, John, and Edward Kaufman, eds., *Second Track/Citizens' Diplomacy: Concepts and Techniques for Conflict Transformation*, Lanham, Md.: Rowman and Littlefield, 2002.

De Hoop Scheffer, Jaap, speech on NATO's role in the Middle East, Israel, February 4, 2005. As of June 14, 2007:
http://www.nato.int/docu/speech/2005/s050224a.htm

Diamond, Louise, and John McDonald, *Multi-Track Diplomacy: A Systems Guide and Analysis*, Occasional Paper No. 3, Grinnell, Ia.: Iowa Peace Institute, June 1991.

Dixit, Kanak Mani, "Within Grasp: Persian Gas for the Southasian Engine," *Himal*, July–August 2005. As of June 18, 2007:
http://www.himalmag.com/2005/july/cover_1.html

Durrani, Mahmud Ali, *India and Pakistan: The Cost of Conflict and the Benefits of Peace*, Oxford: Oxford University Press, 2001.

————, "Pakistan's Strategic Thinking and the Role of Nuclear Weapons," Sandia National Laboratories, Cooperative Monitoring Center Occasional Paper 37, July 2004. As of June 18, 2007:
http://www.cmc.sandia.gov/cmc-papers/sand2004-3375p.pdf

Eisendorf, Richard, ed., *Arms Control and Security in the Middle East*, Washington, D.C.: Initiative for Peace and Cooperation in the Middle East, 1995.

El-Hokayem, Emile, and Matteo Legrenzi, "The Arab Gulf States in the Shadow of the Iranian Nuclear Challenge," Working Paper, Washington, D.C.: Henry L. Stimson Center, May 26, 2006. As of June 18, 2007:
http://www.stimson.org/swa/pdf/StimsonIranGCCWorkingPaper.pdf

Eran, Oded, "Upgrading Relations with NATO," address at the Fifth Herzliyya Conference, Herzliyya Institute of Policy and Strategy, in Hebrew, December 15, 2004.

Euro-Mediterranean Study Commission, homepage, 2006. As of July 18, 2007:
http://www.euromesco.net/

Evangelista, Matthew, *Unarmed Forces: The Transnational Movement to End the Cold War*, Ithaca, N.Y.: Cornell University Press, 1999.

Fahmy, Nabil, "Special Comment," *Disarmament Forum*, United Nations Institute for Disarmament Research, No. 2, 2001, pp. 3–5.

Fatah, Sonya, "Will Opposition from Washington Block a 1,600-Mile Gas Pipeline Connecting Iran, Pakistan, and India?" *Fortune,* December 26, 2005.

Fattah, Hassan M., "Kuwaitis Quietly Breach a Taboo: Easing Hostility Toward Israel," *The New York Times,* October 5, 2005, p. A8.

Fawcett, Louise, and Andrew Hurrell, eds., *Regionalism in World Politics: Regional Organization and International Order,* Oxford: Oxford University Press, 1995.

Feldman, Shai, *Nuclear Weapons and Arms Control in the Middle East,* Cambridge, Mass.: MIT Press, 1997.

Finnemore, Martha, *National Interests in International Society,* Ithaca, N.Y.: Cornell University Press, 1996.

Finnemore, Martha, and Kathryn Sikkink, "International Norm Dynamics and Political Change," *International Organization,* Vol. 52, No. 4, October 1998, pp. 887–917.

Fishman, Alex, "A Moment Before the Iranian Bomb," *Tel Aviv Yedi'ot Aharonot (Leshabat Supplement),* in Hebrew, December 10, 2004, pp. 14, 15.

Funk, Nathan, "Theory and Practice of Track II Diplomacy: Impact and Dynamics of the Search for Common Ground in the Middle East Initiative," doctoral dissertation, American University, Washington, D.C., 2000.

Ganguly, Sumit, "Mending Fences," in Michael Krepon and Amit Sevak, eds., *Crisis Prevention, Confidence-Building and Reconciliation in South Asia,* New Delhi: Manohar, 1996.

Ganguly Sumit, and Ted Greenwood, "Introduction: The Role and Prospects of CSBMs in South Asia," in Sumit Ganguly and Ted Greenwood, eds., *Mending Fences: Confidence- and Security-Building Measures in South Asia,* Boulder, Colo.: Westview Press, 1996, p. 7.

Gibson, James L., "A Sober Second Thought: An Experiment in Persuading Russians to Tolerate," *American Journal of Political Science,* Vol. 42, No. 3, July 1998, pp. 819–850.

Glaser, Charles L., *Analyzing Strategic Nuclear Policy,* Princeton, N.J.: Princeton University Press, 1990.

Griffiths, David, *Maritime Aspects of Arms Control and Security Improvement in the Middle East,* IGCC Policy Paper No. 56, San Diego, Calif.: Institute on Global Conflict and Cooperation, 2000.

Gulf2000, homepage, undated. As of July 18, 2007: http://gulf2000.columbia.edu/

Gulf Research Center, "The Gulf as a WMD Free Zone: Dossier of Official Documents and Statements," undated [a]. (Accessed via the Gulf Research Center homepage, March 14, 2006; hard copy on file with the author.)

————, homepage, undated [b]. As of June 26, 2007:
http://www.grc.ae/

————, *Security and Terrorism Research Bulletin*, No. 1, October 2005. As of June 15, 2007:
http://www.grc.ae/bulletin_WMD_Free_Zone.pdf

————, *Security and Terrorism Research Bulletin*, No. 2, February 2006. As of June 15, 2007:
http://www.grc.ae/data/contents/uploads/Second_Issue%5B1%5D_8044.pdf

Hasan, Khalid, "New Pakistan Ambassador Dubbed General Shanti," *Daily Times*, April 3, 2006. As of June 18, 2007:
http://www.dailytimes.com.pk/default.
asp?page=2006%5C04%5C03%5Cstory_3-4-2006_pg7_33

Heikal, Mohamed, *Secret Channels*, London: Harper Collins, 1996.

Heisbourg, Francois, "The Prospects for Nuclear Stability Between India and Pakistan," *Survival*, Vol. 40, No. 4, Winter 1998–1999, pp. 77–92.

Heller, Mark A., "Arab-Israeli CSBMs: Implications for South Asia," in Sumit Ganguly and Ted Greenwood, eds., *Mending Fences: Confidence- and Security-Building Measures in South Asia*, Boulder, Colo.: Westview Press, 1996, pp. 113–128.

Ikenberry, John, and Charles A. Kupchan, "Socialization and Hegemonic Power," *International Organization*, Vol. 44, No. 3, 1990, pp. 283–315.

Indyk, Martin, "U.S. Policy Priorities in the Gulf: Challenges and Choices," in Emirates Center for Strategic Studies and Research, ed., *International Interests in the Gulf Region*, Abu Dhabi, United Arab Emirates, 2004.

Institute for Multi-Track Diplomacy, homepage, 2007. As of July 18, 2007:
http://www.imtd.org/

Institute for Near East and Gulf Military Analysis, homepage, 2002. As of July 18, 2007:
http://www.inegma.com/

International Institute for Strategic Studies, "The IISS Regional Security Summit: The Manama Dialogue," 2006. As of June 26, 2007:
http://www.iiss.org/conferences/the-iiss-regional-security-summit

International Organization, "International Institutions and Socialization in Europe," Special issue, Vol. 59, No. 4, October 2005.

Jentleson, Bruce, *The Middle East Arms Control and Security Talks: Progress, Problems and Prospects*, San Diego, Calif.: Institute on Global Conflict and Cooperation, 1996.

Jentleson, Bruce W., and Dalia Dassa Kaye, "Security Status: Explaining Regional Security Cooperation and Its Limits in the Middle East," *Security Studies*, Vol. 8, No. 1, 1998, pp. 204–238.

Joeck, Neil, *Maintaining Nuclear Stability in South Asia*, Adelphi Paper 312, London: International Institute for Strategic Studies, 1997.

Johnston, Alastair Iain, "Treating International Institutions as Social Environments," *International Studies Quarterly*, Vol. 45, No. 4, 2001, pp. 487–515.

Jones, Peter, "Maritime Confidence-Building Measures in the Middle East," in J. Junnola, ed., *Maritime Confidence-Building in Regions of Tension*, Washington, D.C.: Henry L. Stimson Center, 1996.

———, "Arms Control in the Middle East: Some Reflections on ACRS," *Security Dialogue*, Vol. 28, No. 1, 1997.

———, *Towards a Regional Security Regime for the Middle East: Issues and Options*, Stockholm: Stockholm International Peace Research Institute, December 1998. As of June 14, 2007:
http://books.sipri.org/product_info?c_product_id=216

———, "Negotiating Regional Security in the Middle East: The ACRS Experience and Beyond," *Journal of Strategic Studies*, Vol. 26, No. 3, 2003.

———, "Arms Control in the Middle East: Is It Time to Renew ACRS?" *Disarmament Forum*, United Nations Institute for Disarmament Research, Issue 2, 2005a. As of June 18, 2007:
http://www.unidir.org/pdf/articles/pdf-art2278.pdf

———, *A Gulf WMD Free Zone Within a Broader Gulf and Middle East Security Architecture*, Dubai, United Arab Emirates: Gulf Research Center, 2005b.

———, "Track II Diplomacy and the GWMDFZ," in Gulf Research Center, *Security and Terrorism Research Bulletin*, No. 1, October 2005, pp. 15–17.

Junnola, Jill R., ed., *Maritime Confidence-Building in Regions of Tension*, Washington, D.C.: Henry L. Stimson Center, 1996.

Kahwaji, Riad, "Political and Security Brief," Institute for Near East and Gulf Military Analysis, February 2006. As of June 15, 2007:
http://inegma.com/politicalsecuritybriefFeb06.htm

Kapur, S. Paul, "India and Pakistan's Unstable Peace: Why Nuclear South Asia Is Not Like Cold War Europe," *International Security*, Vol. 30, No. 2, Fall 2005, pp. 127–152.

Kashmir Study Group, homepage, 2000. As of July 18, 2007:
http://www.kashmirstudygroup.net/

———, "Kashmir: A Way Forward," February 2000. As of June 15, 2007:
http://www.kashmirstudygroup.net/awayforward/wayforward.html

———, "Kashmir: A Way Forward," February 2005. As of June 15, 2007: http://www.kashmirstudygroup.net/awayforward05/wayforward.html

Kasturi, Bhashyam, "India," in P. R. Chari, ed., *Perspectives on National Security in South Asia*, New Delhi, Manohar Publishers, 1999.

Katzenstein, Peter J., ed., *The Culture of National Security*, New York: Columbia University Press, 1996.

Kaye, Dalia Dassa, "Alternative Regional Security Architectures in the Aftermath of Iraq," unpublished RAND research.

———, "IR Theory and the Study of Regions," unpublished manuscript.

———, *Beyond The Handshake: Multilateral Cooperation in the Arab-Israeli Peace Process*, New York: Columbia University Press, January 2001a.

———, "Track Two Diplomacy and Regional Security in the Middle East," *International Negotiation*, Vol. 6, No. 1, January 2001b, pp. 49–77.

———, *Rethinking Track Two Diplomacy: The Middle East and South Asia*, Clingendael Diplomacy Paper No. 3, The Hague: Netherlands Institute of International Relations, June 2005. As of June 18, 2007: http://www.clingendael.nl/publications/2005/20050601_cdsp_paper_diplomacy_3_kaye.pdf

Kaye, Dalia Dassa, and Frederic M. Wehrey, "A Nuclear Iran: The Reactions of Neighbours," *Survival*, Vol. 49, No. 2, Summer 2007, pp. 111–128.

Keck, Margaret E., and Kathryn Sikkink, *Activists Beyond Borders: Advocacy Networks in International Politics*, Ithaca, N.Y.: Cornell University Press, 1998.

Kelman, Herbert C., "Interactive Problem Solving: The Uses and Limits of a Therapeutic Model for the Resolution of International Conflicts," in Vamik D. Volkan, Joseph V. Montville, and Demetrios A. Julius, eds., *The Psychodynamics of International Relationships, Volume II: Unofficial Diplomacy at Work,* Lexington, Mass.: Lexington Books, 1991.

Kheli, Shirin Tahir, *India and Pakistan: Opportunities in Economic Growth, Technology and Security: A Report of the Balusa/Princeton Group*, May 2–4, 1997.

Klotz, Audie, *Norms in International Relations: The Struggle Against Apartheid*, Ithaca, N.Y.: Cornell University Press, 1995.

Kraft, H. J., "The Autonomy Dilemma of Track Two Diplomacy in Southeast Asia," *Security Dialogue*, Vol. 31, No. 3, September 2000.

Kraig, Michael, ed., "Alternative Strategies for Gulf Security," Special issue, *Middle East Policy*, Vol. 11, No. 3, Fall 2004.

Krause, Keith, "Cross-Cultural Dimensions of Multilateral Non-Proliferation and Arms Control Dialogues: An Overview," *Contemporary Security Policy*, Vol. 19, No. 1, April 1998, pp. 1–22.

Krause, Keith, and Andrew Latham, "Constructing Non-Proliferation and Arms Control: The Norms of Western Practice," *Contemporary Security Policy*, Vol. 19, No. 1, April 1998, pp. 23–54.

Krepon, Michael, "A Time of Trouble, A Time of Need," in Michael Krepon and Amit Sevak, eds., *Crisis Prevention, Confidence-Building, and Reconciliation in South Asia*, New Delhi: Manohar, 1996, p. 7.

Krepon, Michael, and Ziad Haider, eds., *Reducing Nuclear Dangers in South Asia*, Report No. 50, Washington, D.C.: Henry L. Stimson Center, January 2004. As of June 15, 2007:
http://www.stimson.org/pub.cfm?id=92

Kupchan, Charles A., "After Pax Americana: Benign Power, Regional Integration, and the Sources of Stable Multipolarity," *International Security*, Vol. 23, No. 2, Autumn 1998, pp. 40–79.

Laipson, Ellen, "Preface," in Michael Krepon and Ziad Haider, eds., *Reducing Nuclear Dangers in South Asia*, Report No. 50, January 2004, Washington, D.C.: Henry L. Stimson Center, p. iii.

Lake, David A., and Patrick M. Morgan, eds., *Regional Orders: Building Security in a New World*, University Park, Pa.: Pennsylvania State University Press, 1997.

Lancaster, John, "India-Pakistan Talks Encourage Both Sides," *Washington Post*, April 18, 2005, p. A10.

Landau, Emily, "Egypt and Israel in ACRS: Bilateral Concerns in a Regional Arms Control Process," Tel Aviv: Jaffee Center for Strategic Studies, Memorandum No. 59, 2001. As of June 18, 2007:
http://www.tau.ac.il/jcss/memoranda/memo59.pdf

———, *Arms Control in the Middle East: Cooperative Security Dialogue and Regional Constraints*, Brighton, UK: Sussex Academic Press, 2006.

Latham, Andrew, "Constructing National Security: Culture and Identity in Indian Arms Control and Disarmament Practice," *Contemporary Security Policy*, Vol. 19, No. 1, April 1998, pp. 129–158.

Lemke, Douglas, *Regions of War and Peace*, Cambridge, UK: Cambridge University Press, 2002.

Leonard, J., S. Limone, A. Aly, Y. Sayigh, A. Sayed, and S. Al-Mani, *National Threat Perceptions in the Middle East*, Geneva: United Nations Institute for Disarmament Research, October 1995.

Lerman, Eran, "Re-Energizing U.S.-Israeli Special Relations," address at the Fifth Herzliyya Conference, Herzliyya Institute of Policy and Strategy, in Hebrew, December 15, 2004.

Levran, Aharon, and Mohammad K. Shiyyab, "A Joint Paper on Jordanian-Israeli Issues of Security and Political Settlement," Washington, D.C.: Initiative for Peace and Cooperation in the Middle East, 1994.

Lynch, Marc, *Voices of the New Arab Public: Iraq, Al-Jazeera, and Middle East Politics Today*, New York: Columbia University Press, 2006.

Makovsky, David, *Making Peace with the PLO: The Rabin Government's Road to the Oslo Accord*, Boulder, Colo.: Westview Press, 1996.

Mann, Richard, "Remarks by His Excellency Ambassador Richard Mann, Canadian Ambassador to Qatar," in David N. Griffiths, ed., *MarSaf 2002 Proceedings*, Ottawa: Canadian Coast Guard, 2002.

Mattoo, Amitabh, "Pakistan," in P. R. Chari, ed., *Perspectives on National Security in South Asia*, New Delhi, Manohar Publishers, 1999.

McDonald, John W., Jr., and Diane B. Bendahmane, eds., *Conflict Resolution: Track Two Diplomacy*, Washington D.C.: Foreign Service Institute, 1987.

McMillan, Joseph, Richard Sokolsky, and Andrew C. Winner, "Toward a New Regional Security Architecture," *The Washington Quarterly*, Vol. 26, No. 3, Summer 2003, pp. 161–175.

Mekenkamp, Monique, Paul van Tongeren, and Hans van de Veen, eds., *Searching for Peace in Central and South Asia*, Boulder, Colo.: Lynne Rienner Publishers, 2002.

"The Memorandum of the State of Kuwait: Observations on the Letter of the Secretary General of the Arab League on Declaring the Gulf Region Free from WMD," December 14, 2005, printed in Gulf Research Center (undated [a]). Original source listed as *Al Hayat*, January 2, 2006.

Meyers, Gayle, ed., *Common Ground on Chemical Risk: Case Studies from the Middle East*, Washington, D.C.: Search for Common Ground, 2003.

Middle East Policy, "Iraq—Gulf/2000 Conference," special section, Vol. 7, No. 4, October 2000.

Moussa, Amr, letter to Abdul Rahman Al Attiya, June 29, 2005, reprinted in Gulf Research Center (undated [a]). Original source listed as *Al Hayat*, January 2, 2006.

Neumann, Iver B., "A Region-Building Approach to Northern Europe," *Review of International Studies*, Vol. 20, No. 1, 1994.

Nolan, Janne E., ed., *Global Engagement: Cooperation and Security in the 21st Century*, Washington, D.C.: Brookings Institution, 1994.

Notter, James, and John McDonald, "Track Two Diplomacy: Nongovernmental Strategies for Peace," *U.S. Foreign Policy Agenda*, United States Information Agency, December 1996. As of June 18, 2007:
http://usinfo.state.gov/journals/itps/1296/ijpe/pj19mcdo.htm

Olster, Marjorie, "Syrian, Israeli Academics Met Secretly in Oslo," *Reuters*, January 2, 1994.

Ortega, Martin, ed., "Global Views on the European Union," Chaillot Paper No. 72, Paris: Institute for Security Studies, November 2004.

Pendharkar, Rajesh, "The Lahore Declaration and Beyond: Maritime Confidence-Building Measures in South Asia," Washington, D.C.: Henry L. Stimson Center, Occasional Paper No. 51, February 2003. As of June 18, 2007: http://www.stimson.org/pub.cfm?id=76

Peres, Shimon, and Arye Naor, *The New Middle East*, New York: Henry Holt and Company, 1993.

Peters, John E., James Dickens, Derek Eaton, C. Christine Fair, Nina Hachigian, Theodore W. Karasik, Rollie Lal, Rachel M. Swanger, Gregory F. Treverton, and Charles Wolf, Jr., *War and Escalation in South Asia*, Santa Monica, Calif.: RAND Corporation, MG-367-1-AF, 2006. As of June 18, 2007: http://www.rand.org/pubs/monographs/MG367-1/

Prawitz, J., and J. Leonard, *A Zone Free of Weapons of Mass Destruction in the Middle East*, Geneva: United Nations Institute for Disarmament Research, February 1996.

Pregenzer, Arian L., Michael Vannoni, Kent Biringer, and Pauline Dobranich, *Cooperative Monitoring Workshop: Focus on the Middle East*, Albuqerque, N.M.: Sandia National Laboratories, May 1995.

Prosser, Ron, "Israel's Atlantic Dimension," *Jerusalem Post*, February 24, 2005.

Pruitt, Dean G., "Ripeness Theory and the Oslo Talks," *International Negotiation*, Vol. 2, No. 2, February 1997, pp. 237–250.

———, "The Tactics of Third-Party Intervention," *Orbis*, Vol. 44, No. 2, Spring 2000, pp. 245–254.

Pugwash Online, homepage, undated [a]. As of July 18, 2007: http://www.pugwash.org/

———, "Consortium of Research Institutes' Project on Regional Co-Operation and Security in the Middle East and North Africa," Web page, undated [b]. As of June 26, 2007: http://www.pugwash.org/reports/rc/me/ME2005/report-july2005.htm

———, "Regional Conflict and Global Security Reports and Statements," Web page, undated [c]. As of June 15, 2007: http://www.pugwash.org/reports/rc/rclist.htm

Qojas, Mazen, *Cooperative Border Security for Jordan: Assessment and Options*, Albuqerque, N.M.: Sandia National Laboratories, March 1999.

Risse, Thomas, "Let's Argue! Communicative Action in World Politics," *International Organization*, Vol. 54, No. 1, February 2000, pp. 1–39.

Risse, Thomas, Stephen Ropp, and Kathryn Sikkink, eds., *The Power of Human Rights: International Norms and Domestic Change*, Cambridge, UK: Cambridge University Press, 1999.

Rizvi, Gowher, *South Asia in a Changing International Order*, New Delhi: Sage Publications, 1993.

Rouhana, Nadim N., "Unofficial Intervention: Potential Contributions to Resolving Ethno-National Conflicts," in Jan Melissen, ed., *Innovation in Diplomatic Practice*, New York: Palgrave, 1999, pp. 111–132.

Rüland, Jürgen, "The Contribution of Track Two Dialogue Towards Crisis Prevention," *ASIEN*, Vol. 85, October 2002, pp. 84–96.

Sagan, Scott, *The Limits of Safety: Organizations, Accidents and Nuclear Weapons*, Princeton, N.J.: Princeton University Press, 1993.

Sandia National Laboratories, *International Security News*, Vol. 4, No. 3, July 2004.

Sandia National Laboratories Cooperative Monitoring Center, homepage, 2007. As of July 18, 2007:
http://www.cmc.sandia.gov/

Saunders, Harold, "When Citizens Talk: Nonofficial Dialogue in Relations Between Nations," in John W. McDonald, Jr., and Diane B. Bendahmane, eds., *Conflict Resolution: Track Two Diplomacy*, Washington D.C.: Foreign Service Institute, 1987, pp. 81–87.

———, "Officials and Citizens in International Relationships: The Dartmouth Conference," in Vamik D. Volkan, Joseph V. Montville, and Demetrios A. Julius, eds., *The Psychodynamics of International Relationships, Volume II: Unofficial Diplomacy at Work,* Lexington, Mass.: Lexington Books, 1991.

———, "Prenegotiation and Circum-Negotiation: Arenas of the Peace Process," in Chester A. Crocker and Fen Osler with Pamela Aall, eds., *Managing Global Chaos: Sources of and Responses to International Conflict*, Washington, D.C.: United States Institute of Peace Press, 1996, pp. 419–432.

Schaffer, Howard B., and Teresita Schaffer, "Kashmir: Fifty Years of Running in Place," in Chester A. Crocker, Fen Osler Hampson, and Pamela Aall, *Grasping the Nettle: Analyzing Cases of Intractable Conflict*, Washington, D.C.: United States Institute of Peace, 2005, pp. 295–318.

Schaffer, Teresita, "India, Pakistan and Kashmir: Of Buses and People," *South Asia Monitor*, No. 81 Washington, D.C.: Center for Strategic and International Studies, April 1, 2005a.

———, *The Economics of Peace Building*, Washington, D.C.: Center for Strategic and International Studies, December 2005b.

Schiff, Ze'ev, Ahmad S. Khalidi, and Hussein J. Agha, *Common Grond on Redeployment of Israeli Forces in the West Bank*, Washington, D.C.: Initiative for Peace and Cooperation in the Middle East, 1994.

Search for Common Ground, homepage, undated. As of July 18, 2007:
http://www.sfcg.org/

———, "Middle East Consortium on Infectious Disease Surveillance (MECIDS)," 2003. As of June 14, 2007:
http://www.sfcg.org/programmes/middleeast/middleeast_mecids.html

———, *Bulletin of Regional Cooperation in the Middle East*, January 2004. As of June 14, 2007:
http: www.sfcg.org/programmes/middleeast/middleeast_bulletin.html

———, "Search for Common Ground in the Middle East: Program Update," October 2006. As of June 14, 2007:
http://www.sfcg.org/Documents/Programs/meupdate.pdf

Sharp, Paul, "For Diplomacy: Representation and the Study of International Relations," *International Studies Review*, Vol. 1, No. 1, Spring 1999, pp. 33–57.

Sick, Gary, and Lawrence Potter, *The Persian Gulf at the Millennium: Essays in Politics, Economy, Security, and Religion*, New York: St. Martin's Press, 1997.

———, *Security in the Persian Gulf: Origins, Obstacles and the Search for Consensus*, New York: Palgrave, 2002.

———, *Iran, Iraq, and the Legacies of War*, New York: Palgrave MacMillan, 2004.

Siddiqa-Agha, Ayesha, "Maritime Cooperation Between India and Pakistan: Building Confidence at Sea," Cooperative Monitoring Center Occasional Paper, November 2000. As of June 26, 2007:
http://www.cmc.sandia.gov/cmc-papers/sand98-050518.pdf

Siddiqi, Toufiq A., "India and Pakistan: Pipe Dream or Pipeline of Peace?" Georgetown Journal of International Affairs, Winter/Spring 2004.

Sidhu, Waheguru Pal Singh, Bushra Asif, and Cyrus Samii, eds., *Kashmir: New Voices, New Approaches*, Boulder, Colo.: Lynne Rienner Publishers, 2006.

Smock, David, ed., *Private Peacemaking: USIP-Assisted Peacemaking Projects of Nonprofit Organizations*, Washington, D.C.: United States Institute of Peace, 1998.

Sokolski, Henry, and Patrick Clawson, eds., *Getting Ready for a Nuclear-Ready Iran*, Carlisle, Pa.: Strategic Studies Institute, U.S. Army War College, 2005. As of June 19, 2007:
http://www.strategicstudiesinstitute.army.mil/Pubs/display.cfm?pubID=629

Solingen, Etel, *Regional Orders at Century's Dawn: Global and Domestic Influences on Grand Strategy*, Princeton, N.J.: Princeton University Press, 1998.

Spiegel, Steven L., "A Report on Enriching the Middle East's Economic Future," brochure for the Conference on Enriching the Economic Future of the Middle East, Doha, Qatar, January 29–31, 2006. As of June 14, 2007: http://www.international.ucla.edu/bcir/doha/pdfs/Brochure.pdf

Stanley Foundation, "The Future of Persian Gulf Security: Alternatives for the 21st Century," Stanley Policy Dialogue Brief, summary of conference proceedings, September 3–5, 2005, Dubai, United Arab Emirates. As of June 14, 2007: http://www.stanleyfoundation.org/publications/pdb/pdb05pg.pdf

———, homepage, 2007. As of July 18, 2007: http://www.stanleyfoundation.org/

"The State of Kuwait: Memorandum Regarding the Position of the State of Kuwait on Declaring the Gulf Region as a Zone Free from Weapons of Mass Destruction," December 14, 2005, printed in Gulf Research Center (undated [a]). Original source listed as *Al Hayat Daily*, January 2, 2006.

Stein, Janice Gross, ed., *Getting to the Table: The Process of International Prenegotiation*, Baltimore, Md.: Johns Hopkins University Press, 1989.

Stewart, Philip D., "The Dartmouth Conference: U.S.-U.S.S.R. Relations," in John W. McDonald and Diane B. Bendahmane, eds., *Conflict Resolution: Track Two Diplomacy*, Washington, D.C.: Foreign Service Institute, 1987, pp. 21–26.

"Syrian, Israeli Academics Met Secretly in Oslo," *Mideast Mirror*, January 4, 1994, p. 9.

Tellis, Ashley J., *India's Emerging Nuclear Posture: Between Recessed Deterrent and Ready Arsenal*, Santa Monica, Calif.: RAND Corporation, MR-1127-AF, 2001. As of June 19, 2007: http://www.rand.org/pubs/monograph_reports/MR1127/

UCLA Ronald W. Burkle Center for International Relations, Conference on Enriching the Economic Future of the Middle East, conference materials, Doha, Qatar, January 29–31, 2006. As of June 14, 2007: http://www.international.ucla.edu/bcir/doha/

United Nations Institute for Disarmament Research, *The Potential Uses of Commercial Satellite Imagery in the Middle East*, Geneva: United Nations Institute for Disarmament Research, September 1999.

———, *Coming to Terms with Security: A Handbook on Verification and Compliance*, Geneva: United Nations Institute for Disarmament Research, July 2002a.

———, *Coming to Terms with Security: A Lexicon for Arms Control, Disarmament, and Confidence-Building*, Geneva: United Nations Institute for Disarmament Research, July 2002b.

United States Institute of Peace, *India and Pakistan Engagement: Prospects for Breakthrough or Breakdown?* Special Report No. 129, January 2005. As of June 18, 2007:
http://www.usip.org/pubs/specialreports/sr129.pdf

U.S. Department of State, Bureau of Political-Military Affairs, "Middle East Peace Process Arms Control and Regional Security (ACRS) Working Group," fact sheet, July 21, 2001. As of June 18, 2007:
http://www.state.gov/t/pm/rls/fs/2001/4271.htm

Vasconcelos, Alvaro, and George Joffe, eds., *The Barcelona Process: Building a Euro-Mediterranean Regional Community*, London: Frank Cass, 2000.

Volkan, Vamik D., Joseph V. Montville, and Demetrios A. Julius, eds., *The Psychodynamics of International Relationships, Volume II: Unofficial Diplomacy at Work,* Lexington, Mass.: Lexington Books, 1991.

Waslekar, Sundeep, "Track-Two Diplomacy in South Asia," Arms Control, Disarmament, and International Security (ACDIS) Occasional Paper, University of Illinois at Urbana-Champaign, October 1995.

Wendt, Alexander, *Social Theory of International Politics*, Cambridge, UK: Cambridge University Press, 1999.

Ya'ari, Ehud, "Rabin's Double Bypass, *The Jerusalem Report*, January 27, 1994.

Yaffe, Michael, "An Overview of the Middle East Peace Process Working Group on Arms Control and Regional Security," in Fred Tanner, ed., *Confidence-Building and Security Co-Operation in the Mediterranean, North Africa and the Middle East,* Malta: University of Malta, 1994.

Yaffe, Michael, "Promoting Arms Control and Regional Security in the Middle East," *Disarmament Forum*, Spring 2001.

———, "The Gulf and a New Middle East Security System," in Michael Kraig, ed., "Alternative Strategies for Gulf Security," Special issue, *Middle East Policy*, Vol. 11, No. 3, Fall 2004, pp. 118–130.

Yaphe, Judith S., and Charles D. Lutes, "Reassessing the Implications of a Nuclear-Armed Iran," Washington, D.C.: Institute for National Strategic Studies, National Defense University, McNair Paper 69, 2005. As of June 19, 2007:
http://www.ndu.edu/inss/mcnair/mcnair69/McNairPDF.pdf

Zarif, Javad, "How Not to Inflame Iraq," *New York Times*, February 8, 2007, p. A21.

About the Author

Dalia Dassa Kaye is a political scientist at the RAND Corporation in Santa Monica, California, and a faculty member at the Frederick S. Pardee RAND Graduate School. She has served as an assistant professor of political science and international affairs at the George Washington University. She has also taught at the University of Amsterdam and has received a variety of awards and fellowships, including from the Council on Foreign Relations, the Brookings Institution, and the Smith Richardson Foundation. She has published widely on Middle East security issues and is the author of *Beyond the Handshake: Multilateral Cooperation in the Arab-Israeli Peace Process*. She holds a Ph.D. in political science from the University of California, Berkeley.